To Judy + John
Sharing my Journey with you!!!

Bud

From Youngstown to Pahokee...

and stops along the way

By Bert Tamarkin

ORAL HERITAGE PRODUCTIONS
Boynton Beach, Florida

Oral Heritage Productions
Boynton Beach, Florida 33437

Copyright © 2007 by Bert Tamarkin

All rights reserved. No part of this publication may be reproduced, displayed, modified or distributed without the express prior written permission of the copyright holder, except in the case of brief quotations embodied in critical articles and reviews. For information, please contact Oral Heritage Productions, oralheritage@bellsouth.net.

Published 2007 by Oral Heritage Productions

Printed in the United States

ISBN 978-0-9791086-0-0

To Finish is to Begin by Michael Monus and personal letter
to Bert Tamarkin by Michael Monus are reproduced by permission

Edited by Patricia Mavo
Book Design by Michael Herbert and Patricia Mavo
Artwork for front and back covers by Michael Lascasas

www.oralheritageproductions.com

To my mother, Pearl, who nurtured me throughout her life and loved me so; and to my wife, and my life, Bernita Ungar Tamarkin, who gave me the inspiration to change my world and to change the direction of my life. For this, I will be eternally grateful. I hope that they would be proud of the work I do and of the book I have written with them in mind.

I am of the opinion that my life belongs to the community... and as long as I live, it is my privilege to do for it whatever I can. I want to be thoroughly used up when I die, for the harder I work, the more I live. I rejoice in life for its own sake. Life is no brief candle to me. It is a sort of splendid torch which I have got hold of for a moment and I want to make it burn as brightly as possible before handing it on to future generations.

– George Bernard Shaw

Table of Contents

Preface vii
Acknowledgments ix
Introduction - What's it all about, Buddy? xi

PART ONE – THE YOUNGSTOWN YEARS
Chapter 1
    My Parents, Pearl Sigel and Jack Tamarkin 3
Chapter 2
    Growing up in Youngstown 12
Chapter 3
    My Years at the Tamarkin Company 28
Chapter 4
    Bernita and Bud, Becoming a Team 32
Chapter 5
    Bernita's Family 44
Chapter 6
    Our Life on Ravine Drive with Jon and Jeff 50
Chapter 7
    Our First Visit to Israel 60
Chapter 8
    Selling the Tamarkin Company and the Saga of Phar-Mor . . . 64

PART TWO – THE PALM BEACH YEARS AND SOCIAL ADVOCACY
Chapter 9
    Creating My Own Identity in Social Advocacy 82
Chapter 10
    Meeting the Needs of Our Senior Population 90
Chapter 11
    Assisting People with Disabilities 96
Chapter 12
    Public Health, Education, and Advocacy 98
Chapter 13
    The Hunger Coalition & the Community Food Alliance . . . 110
Chapter 14
    Being a Social Advocate 116

PART THREE – LOSING BERNITA
Chapter 15
    Fighting a Courageous Battle 120

PART FOUR – CONCLUSION
Chapter 16
    Continuing my Education 144
Chapter 17
    My Eightieth Birthday 148
Chapter 18
    This is what it's all about, Buddy! 154

Preface

When I realized that I was quickly approaching my eightieth year, I began to wonder how my grandchildren would remember me. I see them only a few times a year, during my yearly trip to Youngstown, Ohio, or when they come to Florida to visit. They know me casually and call me "Poppy." In writing this personal history, I hope to give them an opportunity to know their grandparents, Bud and Bernita, and what they tried to accomplish in their lives. This history is also for my sons, Jon and Jeffrey. Although they know me as Dad, in many ways they do not know the person I am today. I want them to understand how their father changed and matured over the past twenty-five years since he left Youngstown. This book is also for the many friends who have encouraged me and supported me throughout the years; particularly those with whom I work. I want you to know that there really is a purpose for the things I do.

The experiences described in this book reflect my own perceptions and my own memories of events. Those who were closely involved in many of the situations described will no doubt have different recollections than mine. They may also have more factual information than I have. Be that as it may, the purpose of this book is to express the ways in which I have personally experienced life events and what I have learned along the way.

I have a strong sense of ethics and moral values that I want to share. When I am no longer a part of this world, I pray that my family will continue to maintain a strong sense of values and be charitable and generous with their time and their finances. Bernita and I tried to live our lives helping others and I hope my family continues this tradition. Enjoy reading this book and getting to know Bernita and me better. If you come away with a deeper appreciation of your family, your potential, and your social responsibilities, then this book will have accomplished what I intended.

Acknowledgments

When I first thought about writing a life history, I discussed the idea with many people. I wish to thank everyone who offered their advice, encouragement, and support. I want to especially thank Patricia Mavo for editing and publishing this personal history. As my friends know, I often ramble on about my favorite subjects and I tend to write in the same manner. Pat kept my writing focused and my thoughts disciplined. I also wish to thank Yvonne Foster who proofread the manuscript and offered many valuable suggestions for its improvement.

Special thanks are extended to my friend, Michael Lascasas, who created the artwork for the front and back covers; and to Michael Herbert, who designed the book's interior layout and helped me finalize some thoughts. I am deeply grateful to my mentor, Becky Gregory, who set a pattern for the discussion on my social advocacy work in Palm Beach County. Although she recently retired and was busy moving to another area, she offered her precious time to assist me. I also owe a great debt of gratitude to Jeanette Hartzell, my co-worker at the Health Department, for all her support and encouragement throughout this endeavor. She was my sounding board.

In the writing of this book, I am sure that I missed many important facts, some very important people, some very good friends, and important incidents. For this, I am sorry. As it turns out, many of the stories presented in the following pages were chosen incidentally. They seemed to best represent the wonderful life I have lived, the fifty-one happy years I had with Bernita, and the wisdom I have gained over the course of a lifetime.

What's it all about, Buddy?

I just arrived home from a wonderful dinner party with some good friends. It is a gorgeous April evening in Palm Beach. The dinner was delicious and the wines were spectacular, as expected in Never-Never Land. We all watch our calories, so I ate only part of the dessert. I said goodnight to my friends and wished them well because they were leaving for various destinations over the next several days. As I was driving home, I passed by Palm Beach Public School and noticed a huge van waiting to transport cars to other parts of the country. The "season" in Palm Beach has come to an end and that means it is time to move on. Our snowbirds will search for new nests in other places, in other worlds. As a permanent resident, I am very pleased with this annual exodus because our traffic lessens, driving on the freeway is easier, and local restaurants are glad to greet us. Summer is a different world here.

I really had a fine time tonight, but on the way home I got to thinking about the way we live and how we often miss the real meaning of our everyday lives. I thought about the way Palm Beachers live in contrast to the way residents in Pahokee live, forty-five miles west of Palm Beach. All of this got me wondering, "What's it all about, Buddy?" With so many people running around constantly and traveling so much, I find myself asking, "Where are we all going and why are we all running so hard to get there?"

I have observed that too many retired friends, despite their former successes and bright minds, choose not to be involved. It seems that these wonderful people don't think of the challenging world in which we live. They feel that whatever they could offer is insufficient or that doing anything positive would be hopeless and a waste of time. Somehow, I have never fit that mold. As I approach this milestone of fourscore years, I find myself wondering, "How did I become the man I am today? Where do I see myself going and why?"

I feel very strongly that those of us who are most fortunate must think rationally and act positively to find solutions for the problems we face as free citizens of the world. We have so many opportunities to make constructive changes. If we continue to let these opportunities pass us by, we may never see them again. We will lose our chance to positively influence future generations. I want to encourage my family, my friends, and other fortunate people, to become more involved in assisting others, particularly those in need within our own communities. I wish to inspire you to find purpose in life, find something that you are passionate about, and be truly charitable. That, in a few words, is the message of this book.

Many thoughts have occurred to me as I approach my eightieth birthday, so I decided that the time had come to put some of these thoughts down on paper. This book gives an account of my family and my growing up in Youngstown, my mentors, my motivations, and all of the things that I have strived to accomplish as a social advocate.

I love my family deeply. I hope that this personal history will help them understand who I am, what I stand for, and what I hope they will attain in their own lives.

Part One
The Youngstown Years

The Youngstown Years

CHAPTER ONE
My Parents, Pearl Sigel and Jack Tamarkin

While reflecting on my early years, I realized that I have been influenced by some very strong people. I am sure that the person who influenced me most was my mother, Pearl Sigel Tamarkin. She was born into a poor family on October 29, 1900. Her father's name was Barney and her mother's name was Betty. We know little about her family's history except that they came to Youngstown, Ohio from Pittsburgh, Pennsylvania during the early 1900s. Both families had previously emigrated from Hungary.

Chapter One

Aunt Sadie Sigel.

Betty and Barney had six children. Pearl was the middle of five daughters. Things were not easy for my mother's family. Pearl and her sisters had to go to work at an early age to provide financial support for the family. The youngest child, Isadore, also known as Joe, was the only boy.

He married Sadie Ginzberg (a classic name) and they had a daughter named Debi. During World War II, he fought in the Battle of the Bulge and his wartime experiences affected him the rest of his life. After many years of struggling, Sadie divorced him, went to work, and raised her daughter Debi on her own. Debi went to my alma mater, the University of Michigan, married, and had two daughters, Kim and Stacy. She later divorced and ran a successful business. She is now remarried and lives in Atlanta.

Ironically, while I was writing this section of my history, I received a phone call from Debi. She told me that Aunt Sadie had just passed away. She was ninety-two years old and was living with Debi and her husband, Frank. Sadie was very close to our family and important to me. I have fond memories of her and all the things we did together. Debi and I spoke for a long time, exchanging stories. She told me that Sadie liked to repeat this one story about me. When I was a teenager, I would go out for an evening and come home and always say, "I had the best time I ever had." This has not changed much. I still love going out, doing things, and being with people. Most of the time I have a ball; if not, I move on.

My mother, Pearl, serving a meal to family members.

My relationship with my mother was very close. She provided continuous and unfailing encouragement all of my life. With my mother, I could do no wrong. She encouraged me to think about new ideas and find different ways to communicate with all kinds of people. She always built me up, in contrast to my sister who bossed me around, or my father who always corrected me. Until the year he died, my father often said to me, "Tell me what you did, and I will tell you what you did wrong."

Pearl always strove for the underdog and worked to make sure that those in need were assisted. She taught me that the normal population could take care of itself and that the underserved poor populations needed extra assistance. They needed to be taught how to be self-sufficient. My mother's philosophy strongly influenced the development of my own personality.

Jack and Pearl at our wedding.

Pearl suffered from health problems most of her adult life. When she had reached the point of serious declining health, my wife Bernita and I, and my sister Fran and her husband, Nate Monus, convinced my father to take her to Las Vegas. She had always wanted to go there, but my father would never take her. Her doctors told us that it was a great idea, as long as she took it easy. So off we went to Las Vegas. In the evenings, we took my parents out for dinner and then returned them to their room. The four of us would then go see a show or gamble.

One night after watching Bernita, Fran, and Nate gamble, I told Bern that I was going back to our hotel room to engage in my preferred Las Vegas activity, which is reading a book. Little did I know that my mother had snuck downstairs to play the slots after my father had fallen asleep. She spied me coming into the casino and hid behind the machines, afraid that I would send her

Pearl enjoyed her trip to Las Vegas. Here we are enjoying dinner together at Caesar's Palace; Nate Monus, Fran, Bernita, Bud, Pearl, and Jack (l. to r.).

Chapter One

My father, Jack Tamarkin

back to bed. She had a great time on that trip and it was wonderful for all of us to be together. She passed away a few months later on July 7, 1972. I was devastated because I loved her dearly.

My father, Jack, was born September 13, 1895 to Morris and Bertha Shifrin Tamarkin who lived in a small Jewish shtetl called Chotchemsk near Kiev, Russia. Our family attempted to locate it, but learned it had been demolished during World War II. My father's mother, Bertha, was supposedly very beautiful and came from a good family that lived in the same shtetl as Morris's family. He wanted to marry her and demanded that she wait until he was able to settle down. She did wait and later they married.

One Jewish family from my grandparents' village, the Ozerskys, had emigrated from Russia to Youngstown and became successful bakers. Because of their success, they encouraged other families from Chotchemsk to come to the United States, including my grandfather Morris who had escaped Russia while serving in the Russian army. Morris came to the United States, sent for Bertha and his two children; my father Jack and his brother Benjamin, and became a food peddler. He eventually opened his own wholesale food company in Youngstown.

A shtetl was a small Jewish village formerly found in Russia and Eastern Europe.

I was told that Morris was the stepson of a large, successful family that treated him badly. When he left Russia and came to the United States, he stayed in contact with only one brother, Nacham, who had also left Russia, but went to live in Palestine.

When I was a very young boy, about six or seven years old, I remember my grandfather receiving an invitation from Nacham to visit Palestine. Because the trip would take a few months, my grandfather went alone. He traveled by ship, aboard the *Rotterdam*. When he returned, we gathered together at my grandparents' home for the traditional Passover seder and my grandfather showed us oranges that had come from an orchard he helped finance in Palestine. The oranges were the size of very tiny fruit. I remember him being so excited and so thrilled about his investment. That memory still remains with me.

Nacham eventually came to the United States and settled in Los Angeles. A couple of years later, he was hit by an automobile while crossing the street and died. He is buried next to Morris and Bertha in Youngstown, Ohio. There are other Tamarkin relatives from my grandfather's family in the United States, but we don't know anything about them.

When Morris and Bertha left Russia and settled in the United States, it was a struggle. By the time my father Jack went to South High School in Youngstown, there were four more mouths to feed in the Tamarkin family. My father had to quit school and go to work. Although he never finished high school, he was very quick and smart, and excelled in math. He always worked too hard and for too many hours his entire life. By the time I was born, he and his partner, Jacob Malkin, an older cousin from Russia, operated two successful grocery stores in Campbell, Ohio, a working class suburb of Youngstown. Their customers were the new immigrants that worked in the local steel mills. My father spoke five languages and was well-respected within the immigrant community.

Eventually things improved in the Tamarkin household and the rest of the children received high school diplomas. There was one girl in the family, Bertha Tamarkin Heselov. The last three boys in the family went to college. Two of the boys, Samuel and Saul, became physicians. Sam was a general practitioner and his patients loved him. Saul didn't have the same bedside manner

Chapter One

Above is a postcard of the original St. Elizabeth Hospital where I was born. My daughter-in-law, Cathy is a nurse in the newly-renovated hospital.

as his older brother, Sam, but St. Elizabeth Hospital in Youngstown liked him very much. When the hospital was expanding, they sent him to Ohio State University to study the new field of radiology. The hospital then assisted him in setting up his own x-ray department within their facility.

The best of the whole Tamarkin lot was my father's baby brother, Uncle Isador (Uncle Iz). He suffered all of his life from rheumatic heart disease and was told that he probably would not live to be fifty years old. He did not marry because he didn't want to leave a young family behind. The entire family always worried about him. He was the greatest joy to all of his nieces and nephews. He did more things for us than our fathers did. He would come to see all of our families every Sunday morning and always brought us something or took us someplace.

Uncle Iz had a group of single male companions who were always together. It was only after he died that all of them married. He was loved and respected by the entire community. I have been told that his were the brains that made the Tamarkin Company a success. He was probably the only real sport in the family. I remember he bought each of the families a silver Lionel electric train set that was the envy of everyone we knew. When he died in his thirties, a great fun part of our growing up was gone.

My father's family was very good to me. Every summer, Uncles Ben, Sam, and Saul invited me to their family cottage on Lake Erie. I would sometimes spend weeks with them and felt like part of their immediate families. My father refused to partner with them on the summer cottage, so I appreciated their warmth and hospitality. They were wonderful to me and being a part of their extended family helped me to have a great childhood.

I was close to my cousins, particularly Arlene, who was near to me in age; and the twins, Jack and Jerry, who later became my business partners at the Tamarkin Company. My other cousins who were close to my age were Phyllis Heselov Wilkoff and her brother, Larry Heselov. Their mother, Bertha, was the only daughter in my father's family and she died at a very early age. Phyllis and Larry were raised by their father and a stepmother.

Summer days at my uncles' cottage were always filled with great fun.

Many years later, we also enjoyed the company of my young cousin, Norman, who was Uncle Saul's son. He was a psychotherapist in Washington D.C. who lived life to the fullest. Norman was a rare bird who had many famous friends and patients. I always had a special spot in my heart for him. On one visit to Washington D.C., Norman joined us for dinner and brought along Eugene McCarthy, the former presidential candidate. McCarthy was a strong liberal who was very interesting to talk with, but after a while it would have been nice for him to let someone else do some of the talking. On another visit to Washington D.C., Norman took me in my navy blue suit to a black tie reception at the Chinese Embassy, at a time when relations were stressed between our two countries.

Cousin Arlene Lockshin.

Before closing this chapter, I want to share with you two family stories about Uncle Saul. He and Zelda had a very romantic life together and retired to Palm Beach where they lived happily until they both passed away. They were always close

Chapter One

My cousin, Jack Tamarkin.

Pictured here at our 50th Wedding Anniversary are Doris Tamarkin (Jack's wife), Jerry Tamarkin, Kay Tamarkin, my son Jon, and Arlene Tamarkin-Lockshin (left to right).

My cousin Debi Wingate with me and Bernita.

to their nieces and nephews. When he was diagnosed with cancer and thought serious medical troubles were beginning, he would not let Aunt Zelda care for him. He didn't want her to suffer. He took a load of pills and never woke up.

Uncle Saul had made me his executor and I retained that position until after my Aunt Zelda died. When their children started bickering about the estate, and no solution could be agreed upon, I left the decision-making up to their lawyers and quit the position.

My Uncle Saul really was a different kind of character. He was different than the rest of his family and was much more sensitive than his brothers. He had a fear about dying and being buried in the ground, so before he retired and moved to Florida, he and Zelda began searching for an acceptable resting place.

They investigated mausoleums throughout the Midwest. He found one that he liked and asked his brothers to become partners. My parents, and Bernita and I, still belonged to a conservative temple and my father was not about to invest his money in his brother's venture at a reformed temple. Uncle Sam and Uncle Ben invested, as did my sister Fran and her husband Nate.

The plan was put in place and the mausoleum was built. Saul, Sam, and Ben decided that they wanted to move their deceased brother and sister, Isador Tamarkin and Bertha Heselov, into the mausoleum. Many years earlier, they had been buried next to their parents in an orthodox cemetery a few blocks away. The officials at the orthodox temple said the bodies could not be moved. They claimed that the only time a body could be moved is if it were to be reburied in Israel. My fancy family didn't like that answer and they argued back and forth to no avail. My family had the chutzpah to sue and take it to court. I couldn't believe it, but the Tamarkin family won the case.

When they opened the two graves, they found nothing but dirt, which they moved as best as they could. Bernita and I used to kid about this story because the family didn't bother to move our grandparents, Morris and Bertha. We would tell people that the children probably thought their parents weren't "top drawer." The irony is that many years later when my Uncle Saul did pass away, he was cremated, as was my Aunt Zelda. Makes a good story though, doesn't it?

THE TAMARKIN FAMILY

Morris Tamarkin — Bertha Shifrin Tamarkin

Jack Tamarkin | Benjamin Tamarkin | Bertha Tamarkin Heselov | Saul Tamarkin | Samuel Tamarkin | Isador Tamarkin

Chapter Two
Growing up in Youngstown

My mother met my father while she was working as a clerk at the Strouss-Hirshberg department store in Youngstown. She married him on April 10, 1921. After one year of marriage, they had their first child, Frances Rae, who was born on September 17, 1922.

When Fran was born, none of my father's siblings were married. She was the first grandchild and shining light of the entire Tamarkin Clan. She was doted on by all of her single uncles. Fran was very cute and very smart, and her dreams and desires all materialized positively throughout most of her life because of her strong determination.

When I was young, I never anticipated that I'd ever be friendly with my sister because our personalities and philosophies were so different. But after I married, she and Bernita became like sisters, and then my friendship with Fran matured. She and her husband Nate were very close to Bernita and me for many years. We did wonderful things together and enjoyed each other's company. Fran was very gracious to us and she always took very good care of her little brother.

Bernita and I with Fran and Nate.

After Fran was born, my mother was advised not to have any more children because it would be too dangerous for her delicate health. She had many medical problems including very bad kidneys. She was devastated and consulted with other doctors who told her that she could possibly have a child if they employed the very new technology of delivery by Caesarean Section. She was thrilled with the opportunity and thought it was worth the gamble. She became pregnant and I was delivered on August 6, 1926.

I was told many times that when I was born the operating room was filled with a multitude of local physicians observing the wonderful Dr. Sherbondy demonstrating the new procedure. It was a serious operation and my mother was unconscious for several weeks. I assume that her unconsciousness was medically induced.

When the time came for my circumcision a week after my birth, my mother was not conscious. When her health returned, she asked what they had named me. They told her, Bertram, and that I had not been given a middle name. Pearl said she hated the name Bertram and was going to call me Buddy instead. I used to tell people that my name was Bertram NMI (no middle initial) Tamarkin.

Well, possibly due to the circumstances of my birth, I didn't progress as quickly as other children. I was born with a large head and didn't walk until I was way past two years old. It took me time to catch up. My mother was extremely patient with me, and was a constant source of encouragement throughout my entire life. My family always kidded me about being a momma's boy and I can remember pictures of me dressed in white clothes until I was six years old. I wasn't fragile, but I was never a rough, tough kid. I established a strong relationship with my mother, who fought so hard to have me. They may have kidded me, but I liked being my momma's boy.

My father and I never had a very close relationship. He worked so many hours every day that he had no time to spend with me. I do know that he was disappointed in me because I was not as smart in school as my sister, nor was I the rugged athlete he wanted me to be. The truth is that we all have our unique qualities and abilities. When my father passed away March 26, 1973, I was upset that I didn't have a stronger relationship with him.

A typical Depression scene.

In 1929, the Depression hit and my father lost everything. During this time, my parents moved from their home on Rush Boulevard to an apartment on the north side of Youngstown. They rented a first floor apartment at 223 Lora Avenue, on the corner of Ohio Avenue. It wasn't wonderful, but this was the Depression, and they had little money and little choice.

My father Jack was an avid investor in the stock market and like other investors at the time, he was highly leveraged on margin and owed a lot of money that he couldn't repay. He co-owned two grocery stores named Malkin-Tamarkin. When the stock market crashed, my father lost his stores and most of his self-respect.

Chapter Two

He had to go to work for his father who then owned a wholesale grocery business called the Tamarkin Company. My father started as an employee and later was able to buy his own share of the company.

Losing the stores was a serious blow. Although he still loved to invest in the stock market, my father vowed that he would never again invest in any stocks that didn't pay a dividend, let alone buy on margin. Many years later, when his younger brother, Dr. Saul, told him about IBM, a new wonderful stock that he and his physician friends were all buying, Jack wanted to know the dividend. When he was told that it was a growth stock with no dividends, he wouldn't invest. Uncle Saul managed to retire to Florida on the money he made from that no-dividend investment.

Our family lived on Lora Avenue until I was eleven years old. I attended McKinley School, which was eight or nine blocks away from our duplex. We walked to school every day. My mother didn't have her own car at that time, and in the event of inclement weather, one of the office boys from the Tamarkin Company would take us to school. Although our neighborhood was ok, duplex living didn't provide the privacy that a growing family needed.

My mother was well-established in the Youngstown community and was very active in Jewish organizations, including the local Women's Jewish Federation and Temple Anshe Emeth Sisterhood. She served as president of both organizations. She was an excellent Jewish cook and frequently gave cooking classes to the young women of the temple sisterhood. She loved to cook and entertain. She and my father were very hospitable. They established a ritual of entertaining people after temple every Rosh Hashanah, the Jewish New Year. Bernita and I continued this practice in Palm Beach, although we didn't cook the food. We did it the easy way and had it catered. My sister Fran, however, had great experience in my mother's kitchen and became an excellent cook of all kinds of foods. Even I learned my way around the kitchen.

Fran's interest in food and nutrition led her to pursue a degree as a registered dietitian. She attended Duke University and graduated from Ohio State University. She did her internship at Michael

Reese Hospital in Chicago. After graduation, she was employed by the Youngstown Hospital Association as a registered dietitian. She quit her job at the hospital when she married and had children, but continued to work as a dietitian on a voluntary basis in the local community.

A few memories of my childhood stand out in my mind. Around 1930, Fran contracted scarlet fever. Our house was quarantined for about eight weeks and I was sent to live with my mother's sister, Aunt Rose Pincus, and her family on the other end of town. After she recuperated from her illness, Fran was left with a very serious case of allergies and asthma. Although money was very tight in our home, she was sent to a specialist in New York City. His name was Dr. Will Cook Spain. He suggested that we spend the winter in Arizona to keep my sister away from the cold, inclement weather.

Seeing the sights in Arizona.

Our trip to Arizona took three days and three nights. We traveled by train. My only memory of the ride was that the private railroad car of the very wealthy Barbara Hutton was attached to our train for a couple of days. We kept staring at it constantly.

I remember our Tucson, Arizona, apartment and the school I attended, but not much more. I enjoyed being there because it was a wonderful new experience. We went to see the old missions in the area, and to Tijuana, Mexico, where I experienced a different language and culture. It was a wonderful adventure for a young boy and my interest in cultural differences continues to this day.

Tijuana, Mexico, 1926.

The summer before we went to Arizona, my mother took our family to Sea Isle City, New Jersey, with her best friends, the Taub family.

Chapter Two

After my sister Fran recovered from scarlet fever, we spent the summer at Sea Isle City in New Jersey with the Taub family. I sent this photo to my dad.

The Lindbergh kidnapping dominated the news.

The doctors felt that the ocean air would be good for Fran's health and they wanted her to be near her physicians in New York City. It was a wonderful summer and eventful as well. While in Sea Isle, I had my first encounter with death. A neighbor, who had been swimming near us in the ocean, remained in the water during an electrical storm and was struck by lightning and died. I will always remember staring at the rescuers as they took the man's body out of the water. That memory of seeing a man's dead body has never left me.

The most frightful incident that haunted me as a child was the kidnapping of Charles Lindbergh, Jr. in 1932. There was so much news on the radio about the baby's kidnapping that it was constantly on everyone's tongue. I was sensitive and at an impressionable age when the kidnapping occurred, only six years old, and it really frightened me. For years after the kidnapping, I always looked under my bed before I went to sleep. I kept thinking, thank God, they caught Bruno Hauptmann.

Overall, my life was an easy one. I always made friends. I had one good friend named Herb Harris who was a great buddy of mine. His family was close to my parents. They owned a restaurant called the Ringside which was located in the downtown area of Youngstown. Together, we worked the dumbwaiter and brought up food from the kitchen. We had many great times over the years.

Although I was a terrible athlete, I made up for it by doing other things. It bothered me that I wasn't athletically inclined, but with no positive encouragement, my interests went off in other directions. I always did pretty well in school and got involved in various kinds of activities. I was always busy and always happy.

I had my bar mitzvah on a very memorable day, September 2, 1939. I will never forget it. That was the day we learned that Hitler had invaded Poland. I will always remember the seriousness of that day because that was when I began to realize what it meant to be a Jew. I was living in a peaceful country, enjoying life. Hearing about the horrible things happening to the Jewish people made me realize how lucky I was to be living in the United States. When our rabbi explained that the situation for the Jews was getting increasingly bleak worldwide, it had a strong effect on me.

Tales of anti-Semitism were often in the newspapers so it wasn't a deep secret that the Jewish people were suffering overseas. Our local paper wrote of the problems facing the Jewish people in Nazi-dominated countries, and in our school we had a few Jewish refugee students from Germany who were being raised by American families. I was one of the students who helped teach the refugees English. It was not until years later that we learned about the atrocities that had taken place in the concentration camps.

Jewish families being rounded up for transport to concentration camps.

The feeling of being Jewish in this strange world affected many of my thoughts. We felt so helpless that something so horrible was happening to people just like us. I thought about the teenagers my age who were living in such circumstances. What would have happened to us if our families had not immigrated to the United States?

By the time I was fifteen or sixteen, the newspapers began talking about the concentration camps. In high school, I became very involved with the Jewish Federation Youth Movement. A junior division was created to help raise funds for Jewish people overseas. My early experiences with this group provided the initial impetus that later shaped my work to assist Jewish people. I often pondered why President Franklin Roosevelt, who had been my family's hero for ending the Depression, didn't do more to help save the Jewish people. Why didn't he bomb the concentration camps or the railroads that were transporting the Jews to their deaths? It

Chapter Two

still makes me believe that Jewish lives were not that important to him. His wife Eleanor would have done much more to save Jewish lives. She was the shining star of the Roosevelt family.

Around this time, despite all of the problems worldwide, my testosterone began to emerge, and my social life began. A local reformed temple, Rodef Sholem, organized a teen group to teach young people social skills, and all of my friends were invited to join. The name of the group was Eleven-Twelve-Thirteen, or ETT.

The group lasted about five years without a name change. I loved that time of my life. I was very social and enjoyed dancing and "jitterbugging." I was a good planner and organizer, and loved to make things "happen." I still do. Fifty years later, those of us who were still living in Youngstown organized the First International ETT Reunion at the Squaw Creek Country Club. We had more than fifty people attend from all over the country, including California and Florida. It was a wonderful nostalgic evening for everyone to come back to the old hometown and rehash old times.

While growing up in Youngstown, music was also a big part of my life. I had years of piano lessons when I was young, but

In 1985, we held our First-Ever International ETT Reunion at the Squaw Creek County Club in Youngstown. We had a wonderful evening talking and laughing about old times. In the group photo are Bert Lockshin and my cousin Arlene Lockshin, Bernita, Lucille Rosenfeld on my lap, and Herb Harris two seats to my left (second row from left).

played rather badly. After I graduated college and came back to Youngstown, I called my old piano teacher, Sophie Slavin, and arranged to take lessons again. My parents weren't happy about me spending time with Sophie and her husband, because they considered the couple much too liberal. My parents knew I was a liberal and thought I was too impressionable. After three or four weeks, Sophie told me that she couldn't believe that I had not developed any technique after all those years of lessons. Much to my parents' relief, that was my last lesson. They no longer had to worry about me becoming a "commie."

I had a good bass voice and was always very involved in singing, both at school and at our Jewish temple. In high school, I sang in a wonderful a cappella choir and was invited to sing in the boy's octet at Rayen High School. We sang all over the city. We were good and I loved it. In my temple, I sang in the choir during the Jewish High Holidays for almost forty years, from the age of thirteen to approximately fifty years old. Singing was always my forte. To this day, when I am at a party and there is someone playing the piano, I will join in singing all the songs of my era, from Cole Porter to Frank Sinatra.

In high school, my grades were good, but not exceptional. My sister Fran was a straight "A" student and co-valedictorian of her high school class. Every year, Fran's former teachers would greet me and say that they expected the same academic excellence from me. I told them not to anticipate that. I never quite lived up to their challenges. My talents were different, but I didn't realize it at the time. When I married Bernita, who had flunked out of so many schools and universities, I realized there was a big difference between book-smart and street-smart. Bernita was street-smart, the kind of smart I'll take every time.

I have fond memories of my high school days, but we were all affected by World War II. We had severe rationing of meat and gas, and no luxuries. And the cigarettes we smoked were awful and tasted horrible. I knew I would be drafted into the service when I turned eighteen, so I decided to obtain some college experience first. I had extra credits in high school, and was told that if I took summer school classes, I could go to college after completing three years of high school.

Chapter Two

The University of Michigan. Striking out on my own.

During my senior year, I applied to the University of Michigan and was accepted. Choosing Michigan was a wonderful decision. I went there alone in 1943, knew no one, and established my own identity for the first time in my life. I knew that the atmosphere there was more intellectual than at Ohio State University, where my family and all of my other friends were going. Going to Michigan was a life-changing experience for me. I credit much of my intellectual curiosity and liberal philosophies to my experiences at Ann Arbor.

As college students, all of my friends and I attended many liberal meetings on campus, including those that featured Walter Reuther, the formidable president of the United Automobile Workers, who discussed the plight of the working man. We also attended meetings organized by the Americans for Democratic Action, which hosted the most liberal thinkers from around the world, including some from Russia. Although we attended these meetings, none of us wanted to become communists and we never joined the Americans for Democratic Action. Luckily, my name was not on the list of communist sympathizers which was compiled during the McCarthy hearings. My father would have killed me. Many years later, however, whenever someone presented a liberal pitch or a new community initiative to help the poor, my partners at the Tamarkin Company would send the person to me. They always told everyone that I was their "company communist."

In January of 1945, after my eighteenth birthday, I was drafted. I didn't want to be drafted into the Army's infantry; and fortunately, I was accepted by the Navy. I went to Great Lakes Naval Training Center where I attended boot camp for seven weeks. Several of the guys who were drafted with me came from Brier Hill, the toughest neighborhood near my high school. I didn't know them very well, but they knew me, and all of them became my protectors. No one was allowed to talk badly about their friend, the "little Jew boy." With their support, I had no problems during those seven weeks and I was probably the only Jewish person in my section.

The Navy gave everyone a series of aptitude tests, and since I had received pre-med training, I was assigned to the Naval Hospital Corps School in San Diego, California. However, a medical complication developed before I left for San Diego. I had contracted the mumps. I was hospitalized for over a month and was bedridden for twenty-eight days. The virus had descended into my testicles, which swelled badly. As a result, my sperm count went down to a very low number, which ultimately affected my future reproductive capabilities.

Great Lakes Naval Training Center, circa 1940.

While attending the Hospital Corps School, I was seated in front of a bright young man named John Mayo Tanner. John was from Ashland, Kentucky, a real redneck part of the country. We would talk sometimes about the homework we were doing, but that was the extent of our contact. It was a very cool relationship. About six weeks after we met, he told me that he had something to discuss with me. He said he had always been taught terrible things about Jewish people. He had never met a Jewish person before and he couldn't understand why I wasn't different than he was. That was the beginning of a wonderful relationship. We became best friends while stationed together in San Diego and then at the Naval Hospital in Philadelphia. He later became a physician in Nashville, Tennessee, and Bernita and I visited him and his wife when we attended the Chattanooga World's Fair.

I was drafted into the Navy, January 1945, at the age of eighteen.

Hospital Corps School was very interesting. It was wonderful being in California and we managed to get away on a couple of overnight visits to Los Angeles and Hollywood. For a bunch of eighteen-year-old Midwesterners, it was very exciting.

Chapter Two

Company 44–2, U.S. Naval Hospital Corps School, June 2, 1945. Third row, second from right, Pharmacist's Mate 3rd Class, Bud Tamarkin.

My family was friendly with a former Youngstown couple who lived in California, Sophie and Abe Levin. The Levins were friendly with the Warner Brothers, who were born and raised in Youngstown. Annie Warner Robbins was a frequent visitor to Youngstown and was a friend of my mother's. The Levins were wonderful to us when we visited. They took us to the Warner Brothers Studio. We also had lunch in the actors' lunch room, looked at the movie stars, and enjoyed some wonderful rubbernecking while we were there.

About the time that I was finishing hospital corps training, the war in Europe came to an end. The war in the Pacific continued, however, and we didn't know if we would be assigned to the Marine Medical Corps operating in the South Pacific. It was a very nervous time for us. Luckily, our entire group was sent to the Philadelphia Naval Hospital in South Philadelphia. Man, that was a happy time when we were given our orders. We sure did celebrate.

I graduated from Hospital Corps School as a Pharmacist's Mate 3rd Class. We then had to take a terrible and tedious ride on a troop train from San Diego to Philadelphia. We had three-level-bunks and the thing I remember most was that the ride was unending. Our train was diverted and sidetracked several times from one place to another. A war was on and we weren't a priority. We were on that train for four or five days. We did get to stop in New Orleans and were given a brief pass to see the city. Naturally, we went to the bars and the Latin Quarter. The locals were pushing some drink with a fancy name that was a mixture of champagne and liquor. It was good going down, but it wasn't so good coming up. I don't think I was ever that sick in my entire life, but we sure did have a blast.

When we arrived at the Philadelphia Naval Hospital, we were given floor duty on the wards. The hospital was a center that received sailors and marines who had been injured overseas. My assigned ward was a pre-amputee and post-amputee ward, with about forty to fifty men. After two days on the floor, I was placed alone on night duty. One of my responsibilities was to give penicillin shots to each patient every four hours. The needle seemed as big as I was. Some of these men had received so many shots that it was difficult to find a place to insert the needle. I found this work so upsetting that I had to figure out a way to get a new assignment.

About two months later, I was advised that there was an opening in the ward that rehabilitated sailors and marines who were newly blinded. They were looking for someone who could teach typing and assist the men with social skills. Although I happened to be a terrible typist, with only six weeks of lessons, I applied for the job. I was desperate to get out of the wards giving penicillin shots, and I employed all of my personable skills to land the position.

I was lucky and was hired. It was one of those great experiences in which you learn how to deal with different kinds of people, especially people with disabilities. As one of their instructors, I learned the importance of showing respect instead of pity. Along with the other staff, we taught these men the skills they would need to cope with their blindness and their lives after they left the hospital. This approach of helping others to help themselves continues to be one of my core beliefs.

One of our duties was to take our patients out to eat dinner and to see a movie or a play. We sat with them and taught them how

Chapter Two

to eat in public, we explained what was happening in a movie or play, and we helped the patients develop new socialization skills. It was specialized training and suited my personality and skills perfectly. I loved it. I even received some college credit for the work I did. The sad part was that some of these men had become blind because they drank the wrong kind of alcohol (methanol or wood alcohol) that they had found and imbibed illegally while in the service. What a terrible price they had to pay for a few moments of pleasure in a war zone.

While I was in the Navy, I never served overseas. I was stationed in Philadelphia the entire time. When I was drafted, my father insisted that I take out a war bond from my pay. In those days, sailors made about $30.00 every paycheck. The bond purchase made me continually strapped for cash. I washed and ironed my own uniforms and rarely went out. I could hardly make it to the next pay period. When my mother and sister came to visit me, Fran called our father and insisted that he put me on an allowance to make up for the bond purchase. Naturally, he listened to her, and my life got much better from then on. Only Fran could make my father change his mind.

On my nineteenth birthday, August 6, 1945, the atomic bomb was dropped over Hiroshima, Japan. The war was finally coming to an end. I was retained in the service about fifteen more months and was discharged after serving approximately twenty-one months. I returned home and re-enrolled at the University of Michigan. There was a wonderful post-war attitude that prevailed in the country. Everyone took advantage of the GI Bill of Rights and our college education cost us very little money. What a difference compared to today's world.

I belonged to a great fraternity, Zeta Beta Tau. The atmosphere at the University of Michigan was very intellectual and very liberal. Classes were very difficult and homework was sometimes overwhelming. It was great training for all of us. Most of my friends loved and learned to appreciate music, and we attended concerts frequently. The exposure to classical music made a lasting impression on all of us.

Michigan was a small school at the time and our college life was wonderful. I loved every minute of it. Many of the friend-

Zeta Beta Tau. Attending the University of Michigan was a life-changing experience for many of us.

ships I established there have lasted a lifetime. In the fall of this year, I am attending a reunion with my fraternity friends. One of my fraternity brothers and former roommate, Allan Bratman, lives in Palm Beach and we belong to the same country club. We see each other often, especially at concerts. I have remained close with another college roommate, Al Harris, who lives in Chicago. Since Bernita passed away, he calls me, and another friend who is ill, every Sunday morning. I told him that it was ok if he didn't call, but I think the contact with me is an important part of his life.

When we returned to college after the service, eight of us wanted to have a reunion to celebrate our safe return, so I invited my friends to Youngstown for the New Year's holiday. I think the main reason they wanted to come to Youngstown was to meet my grandfather, Morris, who was eighty years old and still going strong with his long-term mistress.

Eighty years old seemed like a world away at the time for all of us (it is hard to believe it is happening to me now.) When my grandmother Bertha lost her two children, Bertha and Uncle Iz, she became a recluse and withdrew from society. I think that's part of the reason for my grandfather's behavior.

His girlfriend was a married Jewish woman with a family who belonged to his temple, where he was president for too many years. They were seen together in

Here I am with college friends, Al Harris (left) and Bill Berman (center).

Chapter Two

public all the time. My friends thought he should be our idol. We did kid about it for a long time. It is interesting to note that after he died, the Tamarkin family realized that there was no money left in his estate to disburse to his family. Wasn't that a shock?

There is a funny story associated with my grandfather's mistress. She had a son who was a police officer in Youngstown. Over the years, Bernita had acquired numerous traffic tickets, which she hid in the glove compartment of her car. She would never admit to them or tell me about them. One night, a searchlight shined on our apartment and a police officer arrived at our door with an arrest warrant. We asked his name and found out he was the son of my grandfather's lady friend. Well, Bernita invited him in for a cold drink and we talked and laughed with him about our families for a long while. We gave him a check to pay for Bernita's tickets and whenever we saw him in the future, we would always laugh about that night. After all, he was family.

In the days after the war, all single men returning from college lived with their parents. No one had his own apartment. This was the postwar period and housing was at a premium, even in Youngstown. By then, I had become a little bit of a snotnose. I felt that I had grown far above my family intellectually. I spent all of my time either working at the office or in my room listening to records on a record player built to my specifications. It was the ugliest thing you ever saw, but it was my best friend at the time.

I had no money for a car because I was working for my father at a very low salary. He insisted that I share his car, an exceptionally ugly Dodge coupe. I ended up taking the bus to work for over a year until he found it acceptable for me to have a car of my own at the age of twenty-two.

By that time, my sister had married Nate Monus, a Youngstown boy, whose family was very successful. His father was an entrepreneur with a foreign accent who was involved in real estate and a chain of women's hat shops. While they were in high school and long before Nate went into the service, Fran and he plotted out their future. Fran kept saying that she and Nate were going to live life and enjoy it to the fullest, and not live the way their families were living. I know she passed up many potential suitors. I recall my mother arguing with her to keep her options open, but she waited for her Nate. Soon after he returned from the service, Fran and Nate married. They had two children, Mickey and Susan, and were married for over fifty years.

Downtown Youngstown in its heyday.

Youngstown was once home to a thriving steel industry.

Chapter Three
My Years at the Tamarkin Company

When I was choosing a career for myself, I had no major decision to make. My father told me I had two choices, either be a physician like my uncles or go to work at the Tamarkin Company. A medical career was not a possibility; I hated blood. So I joined my father and Uncle Ben at the Tamarkin Company.

I first started working at the company while I was in high school during the early years of World War II. Most of the company's young employees were in the service, so I assisted in the office after school and during summer vacations. My career at the Tamarkin Company started as an office boy.

After graduating college, I was doing the same kind of work at the company that I had done before I went to college. I was miserable. I realized that I would have to demand an acceptable position for myself. My Uncle Ben didn't respect a younger influence any more than my father did. I took many years of negative feedback from them until I started fighting back. One day, I stated my position to both my uncle and my father, and I stopped backing down. I was not going to spend my life as an office boy. I had always been respectful of them, but the time had come for me to demand some respect. It wasn't easy. I insisted on more responsibilities, and eventually, I took an executive position, working next to my uncle in the purchasing department.

My father and Uncle Ben never got along well. They were always bickering with each other. My father was very unsophisticated and never tried to improve himself. He worked hard, liked what he did, and had no interest in changing his routine. He ran the warehouse very well and stayed away from the front office and the management. Even though he was very smart, he permitted my uncle to make too many of the business decisions.

The first Tamarkin warehouse.

Approximately eight years after I joined the company, Uncle Ben brought his twin sons, Jack and Jerry, two fine young men, into the business. They had graduated from Cornell University with engineering degrees and served as officers in the Army. My brother-in-law, Nate, also joined the company at approximately the same time. The Monus family company he had been running was not doing well.

As the Tamarkin Company grew, we left our antiquated and inefficient six-floor building in downtown Youngstown and built a warehouse on the outskirts of town, at 555 North Meridian Road. With additional space, we were able to create a more modern operation. We added a very large IBM order processing machine, which took up an entire room. It was a tremendous change for us and very different from the type of smaller equipment used today. Jerry joined the buying and merchandising staff, and Jack worked in the warehouse with my father. Nate became our financial manager.

About ten or fifteen years after moving to the Meridian Road location, we were again bursting at the seams. We commissioned a new building at 375 Victoria Road, Austintown, that was three times as large as the original facility. This building is still used today by our successors. It is owned jointly by all our children and the Giant Eagle principals who purchased the Tamarkin Company.

My father Jack and Uncle Ben were equal partners in the Tamarkin Company. I was a junior partner along with Jack, Jerry, and Nate. We would all inherit the company equally after their retirement. After a few years working as junior partners, the four of us approached the senior Tamarkins and told them that there was no future for us in the wholesale grocery business if we continued to operate according to our old business methods. Our customers, the small independent grocery stores, were losing their share of the market to the larger and more popular

Chapter Three

supermarket chains. We needed to open up our own supermarkets to compete with powerful competitors like the A&P, Kroger, Loblaw, and a locally-owned chain called Century Super Markets.

The senior partners were not happy with this discussion. They did not want to borrow money to start something new that was unproven. They believed that we should stay in the business we already knew or go into a different field. Nonetheless, they did realize that there was merit to our arguments. After discussing the plan with each of us individually, they finally agreed and said, "Ok, do what you think you have to do, but do us a favor and don't tell us about it." That was the beginning of the new Tamarkin Company, which became very successful.

One of my favorite stories about the Tamarkin Company involved my father Jack. As I mentioned earlier, Uncle Ben ran the office and my father ran the warehouse. My father did the hiring, the deliveries, and worked with the warehouse employees. He worked like a dog from 6:30 a.m. to well after 6:00 p.m. When we modernized, my cousin Jack assumed charge of the new, more complicated and mechanized warehouse. After my father had gotten up in years, he continued to maintain his regular work schedule at the company every day. He kept himself busy working with the warehouse men and managing the returns and salvage operations, and he dressed appropriately for that kind of work. One day, I overheard a couple of salesmen talking. They were saying how nice it was that the Tamarkin Company gave that old man a job. When we heard the story, we all laughed and told the salesmen not to feel too badly because that old man owned the company!

Our new grocery stores were named Valu King. This is another great tale. When we first started our chain of supermarkets, we thought that the name Food King was a winner. After our lawyer conducted a national trademark search, he gave us his approval. We ordered very large signs shaped like a crown which had spaces for four letters on top (FOOD) and four letters on the bottom (KING). Then, within days of opening, we were sued for using someone else's trademark name. We certainly had some fine lawyer. Well, the signs with the crowns were already installed and we had to come up with a new name that worked with the four-letter spacing. We came up with the name Valu King without the "e" and this became our new symbol.

Those were wonderful years for our family. We were all very fortunate. We kept reinvesting and modernizing our business and became more successful as the years went on. Part of the reason for our success was that we four partners, Jack, Jerry, Nate, and I, all got along so well. Whenever we attended national meetings, other companies couldn't understand how we family members could work together so cooperatively and be so successful without one of us being solely in charge. We would explain that part of our success was that we didn't have interfamily problems and that our company was continually growing. We asked our families not to interfere with our business operations. We asked that they respect our decisions and remain friendly with each other. We four partners had lunch together every day in our office and if there were any problems, we discussed them immediately and found solutions. The company did well, everyone profited, and we all lived a good life.

After we sold the business and I later retired to Palm Beach, I would sometimes think about all the years I spent at the Tamarkin Company. My Palm Beach life and the work I was doing in social advocacy became so fulfilling that I would sometimes comment to Bernita, "I should have started my social service career much earlier than I did, rather than having spent all those years working at the Tamarkin Company." She would remind me that "we and our children would not have lived this wonderful life if you spent your entire career in the social service field." That was very true; and when we sold the company, I was able to create a whole new life for myself, a life devoted to social service and the things I held most important.

Chapter Four
Bernita and Bud, Becoming a Team

After the war ended, I returned home and graduated from college. There was no social life for singles in Youngstown, so a group of us began a social club for Jewish singles who had recently returned from college and from the war. I have always been an organizer, so I became very involved in forming the group. We named it YAG, the Young Adult Group. We invited single Jewish people from Warren, Ohio; and Sharon and New Castle, Pennsylvania to join since these cities were less than fifteen miles from Youngstown. The group was very successful and we had a ball.

YAG had more than one hundred members. We planned a variety of social activities and gave bridge lessons to everyone. We scheduled dance classes for the membership and hired a young married couple we knew from the Arthur Murray dance studio to teach us the jitterbug, rumba, tango, and all of the popular dances. The class was so large that a few of us who knew how to dance became assistant teachers. One of the members who came to the dance classes, but never advanced too much as a dancer, was Bernita Ungar. She was then, as she was always, the life of the party. Everyone who knew her loved her.

YAG was very active for a few years, arranging bus trips and visiting interesting places in our area. Because of this group, at least ten couples connected and were married, including Bernita and me. Our families belonged to the same temple and knew each other from mutual involvement in the grocery business. To me, Bernita, this tomboy who I watched grow up, was not really my style. I was the self-styled, pseudo-intellectual, and she was the athletic type. After we were married, I used to laugh when people would say to me, "Buddy, you're hitting the golf ball almost as far as Bernita does!"

Growing up, I had many girlfriends. My first girl, Lucille Rosenfeld, lived in Youngstown. I went with another wonderful girl, Margie Zaller from Toledo, while I was attending the University of Michigan. Bernita had her boyfriends, too, although her father would never have approved of most of them. We both had very active social lives while growing up. Shyness was never part of our natures.

Although Bernita and I were different, we also shared many similarities. We both loved people and we were both extroverts.

Chapter Four

We were also charitable and had a very strong sense of morality and purpose.

During our years with YAG, we found ourselves on the same wavelength most of the time. We were thrown together often, and after a couple of years of being friends, we started dating each other, but not exclusively. We became engaged the night before New Year's Eve of 1952, and were married on March 22, 1953 in a huge wedding at our temple and country club. We honeymooned for three weeks in the Caribbean and began a wonderful life together.

When Bernita and I were engaged, our rabbi, Leonard Azneer, gave us a lecture that he provided to all future brides and grooms. He discussed how we came from two of the most prominent families in town and then added that we were also the two most spoiled kids in town. In his opinion, our chances of having a successful marriage were very slim and we would need to work hard to make the marriage last.

Well, our first year of marriage was only mildly unpleasant. I told Bernita a number of times that her father was not going to pay her outrageous bills anymore, and she replied that it would be ok for me to spend some of the money I kept squirreling away. We soon realized that our life together was very good and that we were very lucky. Despite our earlier disagreements, we learned to adjust to each other and developed a relationship that was the envy of everyone we knew. By the way, Rabbi Azneer's marriage ended in divorce.

Earlier, I described the positive influence my mother had on me. She was my mentor and biggest supporter, and she filled an important role in the early part of my life. When I married, Bernita took over, and became the next, and greatest, positive influence of my entire life.

Bernita was the first person who really helped me develop a strength of character, which is the essence of who I am today. From the beginning, Bernita strove to give me the confidence I needed to achieve my goals. She helped me realize that I had not yet reached my true potential. After we married, the two of us established our own identity and friends, outside of the identity we had previously.

Bernita had a way of assessing people and of gaining their confidence. She instilled this sense in me. She would meet people, assess them in her own way, and then set a direction for her future relationship with them. She always said that her first impressions were right and that she made very few mistakes in judgment.

According to Bernita, I was a terrible judge of people. She said I was too trusting and that people took advantage of me, which was probably true. I would judge everyone positively at first, although Bernita might not. She was right about people many more times than I, and we always laughed about it. She taught me that just because something shines, it doesn't mean it's gold or silver; it might just be a lot of brass.

Bernita also taught me to rely on my own judgment. She reminded me to study something carefully, make my own decision, and not be swayed by a lot of glitz. She was the person who encouraged me to go in my own direction. I had always gone along with what everyone else wanted to do. That was all right with me for many years, but it was not very fulfilling. She taught me that I didn't have to please everyone and that I would be much happier and more satisfied if I trusted my own instincts and acted upon them.

I thought about this a few weekends ago. Since I had many expensive plans for my eightieth birthday year and was spending so much money on family and vacations that year, I thought that I might forego my spring trip to New York City, which I had been taking since I graduated college (the cheap-assed bastard again). I woke up that night and thought of Bernita and said, "What's the matter with me? I shouldn't pass up one of my great yearly joys at this age." I got up early the next morning and

Bernita was always the life of the party and always insisted on being glamorous, as shown above.

Chapter Four

Beverly Sills' debut at the Met in 1975.

A visit to New York is not complete without seeing a performance at the Met. On one memorable opening night, Bernita and I met and spoke with Mrs. Douglas MacArthur.

made my plane and theatre reservations.

I could have spent time with friends while I was in New York, but I wanted to do what I am unable to do in Florida, such as going to the theatre and visiting some NYC public schools. I took *Team of Rivals,* my big eight-hundred-page book on Abraham Lincoln by Doris Kearns Goodwin, and that was my companion during dinner and theatre intermissions. I checked on some education programs at two different progressive public middle schools in the city, learned a great deal, and enjoyed myself immensely.

I am a real New Yorkophile. I read the New York Times daily; Tom Friedman is my idol. I crave good serious New York theatre. I like to see contemporary art and new artistic places that have been constructed in the Big Apple. After we married, Bernita always accompanied me on my trips to New York. I would go see new unusual things or some classical theatre, and Bernita would go shopping or out with the girls.

One of my favorite experiences in New York is to see a performance of the Metropolitan Opera at Lincoln Center. Whenever we took our yearly trip, I always wanted to attend the opera.

After two years of forcing Bernita to enjoy the performance, I gave up. She would always make me walk out after two acts, commenting that they were all going to die anyway. I gave in unhappily and began attending Saturday matinee performances alone.

My best story about the Met was when I obtained tickets for the season's opening night and the debut of Beverly Sills. We arrived early to watch the

36 Bernita and Bud, Becoming a Team

famous pre-opera show when people arrived adorned and wished to be noticed. As we were standing in the lobby, Bernita, who never forgot a face, saw a woman who looked familiar and she said, "Hello, Mrs. MacArthur." The woman was Mrs. Douglas MacArthur, widow of the late General Douglas MacArthur, the Supreme Commander of the Allied Forces in the Pacific during WWII. She stopped and talked with Bernita, sharing stories about her life with a famous man. The following night, we were attending a play and when we walked into the theatre lobby, Mrs. MacArthur was there and called out to Bernita, "Young lady from Ohio, come and talk to me."

From the first winter that Bernita and I wintered in Palm Beach, we had season tickets for the local Regional Arts Concert series. I insisted upon it if I were to spend so much time in Palm Beach. I loved music and part of our agreement was going to include concerts. After several years of trudging along to the performances, Bern began to develop the "blue flu" about an hour before the concerts were to begin.

I finally made a deal with her. I would go to the concert with a wonderful widow friend of ours, Helen Bank, and Bernita could stay home. We would all go out to dinner together, but we'd drop Bernita off at home before Helen and I left for the concert. For a few years, people asked me where Bernita was, but then they stopped asking. She was happy, and I was happy that she wasn't spending the entire concert leafing through the program looking at the names of contributors.

I had served on the Youngstown Symphony Board for many years, and when I was rotated off, Bernita was asked to serve. Everyone kidded her about being on the board and having to attend all the concerts. She loved being on the board because she could meet the artists and help the symphony with social affairs. When Benny Goodman came to play a pop concert with our local symphony, we hosted a reception after the concert at our home. That social aspect of the symphony is what she loved and it was a great part of our social life in a small town.

I have always loved serious movies, documentaries, and especially foreign films. Naturally, Bernita hated them and complained bitterly if I insisted she see a film with subtitles. So I got into a routine on Saturdays where I would play golf, have lunch with my

Chapter Four

foursome, and then go see a foreign film at the Carefree Theatre in West Palm Beach. When I was preparing to leave, Bernita would call me over to her lunch table and tell her friends that her "Pee Wee Herman" was going home to get his raincoat and go to the art films. Bern and her lunch friends always waved and said, "Bye, Pee Wee."

Bernita never enjoyed the culture I savored. She didn't like to read unless it was a specific book about some special person she knew or admired. However, she loved to read a book if it contained an explanation of a stock issue. Bernita loved the stock market. She never passed up a Wall Street Journal, which she read daily. It was her bible. She studied the stocks and the stock market constantly. I never had her sense of intuition and was never any good at choosing stocks or making a profit in the market. Bernita loved it so much that I relinquished that part of our lives to her.

She hated to lose money in a stock and would retain them much longer than she should have. It was always a fight to have her sell stock at a loss. We never did badly or lost a large amount of money, but we were never real winners either. Our lifestyle was provided by our business and not by our investments. I was not a gambler or risk-taker; my father scared that out of me when I was very young when he found a few of us playing dice in the garage. I think that cured me for life.

In addition to her love of the stock market, Bernita loved her sports. She was a good tennis player and a good golfer. She was very competitive.

Bernita had a mind that was always questioning. She could be very stubborn and very convincing when she took a stand

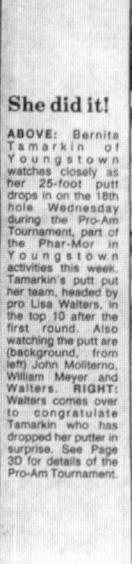

She did it!
ABOVE: Bernita Tamarkin of Youngstown watches closely as her 25-foot putt drops in on the 18th hole Wednesday during the Pro-Am Tournament, part of the Phar-Mor in Youngstown activities this week. Tamarkin's putt put her team, headed by pro Lisa Walters, in the top 10 after the first round. Also watching the putt are (background, from left) John Moliterno, William Meyer and Walters; RIGHT: Walters comes over to congratulate Tamarkin who has dropped her putter in surprise. See Page 3D for details of the Pro-Am Tournament.

Tribune Chronicle

on an issue. The following "Arby's Story" is a good example of this.

In Youngstown, we were good friends with Leroy Raffel and his wife, Shanky. Leroy and his brother, Forrest, owned a restaurant equipment business that hadn't been very successful so they came up with the idea to create and franchise a fast-food roast beef sandwich chain called Arby's. I couldn't understand why anyone would want to go to a restaurant that only offered one item, but the Raffel brothers thought differently. One day, they invited their friends to come to a roast beef sandwich tasting. We attended and liked it. The roast beef was very good, but we really weren't fast-food customers.

Leroy and Forrest opened their first Arby's restaurant in Boardman, Ohio, an upper-class suburb located near the first successful McDonald's restaurant in our area. Contrary to our predictions, they did great business which enabled them to open up a second store not far from our home in Youngstown. This restaurant also did well. Then the Raffels invited six of their good friends to invest in an Arby's franchise plan. They asked for an investment of $25,000 each and the investors together would own a franchise for the next six Arby's that were going to be built. I thought it was a good deal and so did our family, all but Bernita.

She said that she had been taught never to invest in friends' businesses. Furthermore, she added, not even the Raffels' mother was investing her money in her sons' project. Bernita said she liked the Raffel boys personally, but would not invest her money with them. She managed to convince us, so no one in our family pursued the investment. About three years later, when Arby's was still expanding, one of our cousins, Bert Lockshin, came up to Bernita at a family party and told her that it was her fault that none of us ever shared in the bounty that the Raffel brothers had created. She shook her head and said that she was sorry.

As it turned out, the Raffels kept

Our friends, the Raffel brothers, founded the fast-food chain known as Arby's.

Chapter Four

expanding the Arby's franchise and eventually, the bottom fell out of the fast-food business. They had expanded too fast in too many bad locations and the company went bankrupt. Of course, Bernita couldn't wait for the next family dinner to see Bert Lockshin and show him how smart she was.

The bankrupt company was placed under a new management team and had a couple of bad years. Leroy Raffel was frustrated with the new operation and told the management that he could bring his company back to life again and he would do it for no salary. Instead, he requested stock options for himself and his brother, Forrest. Management accepted, and Leroy made the company very successful again. The Raffels recouped their investment, sold the stock, and retired to Florida. The few original investors who had stayed with the company made a serious amount of money.

Bernita and I had a wonderful group of friends in Youngstown. Two of our good friends were Ada and Irwin Thomases. They had moved to Youngstown with their two daughters from Jamestown, New York. They bought a home in the Jewish section of town and joined the country club. Irwin was in the shopping center business and originally came from New York City.

Ada and Irwin were both intelligent people, well-read, and very liberal activists. I particularly appreciated their liberal personalities. Within a couple of years, they established a group of about five couples that spent a lot of time together. The group consisted of the Thomases, the Raffels, the Zeves, the Speros, and Bernita and me.

Ada was a real spitfire activist. She was very outspoken and would not suffer idiots. She was certainly different, but to those who knew her, she was a real joy. Ada loved to entertain and had dinner parties for her "group" every couple of weeks. The food was never very good and we would laugh about her new food creations from Woman's Day, a magazine she bought at the A & P supermarket. Before dinner, we would all have a couple of drinks, martinis being the rage of the time, and then we would sit down to dinner and eat while everyone would argue and scream loudly about politics.

Ada decided after several months that we were all getting out of hand. She said we were becoming alcoholics and it wasn't becoming to any of us. She told us that we were invited to dinner the next weekend, but we would only be allowed two drinks. We would then have a nice calm dinner with no alcohol. We went to their home, had our two drinks, sat down for dinner, and argued just as loudly without the extra alcohol. She gave up and we all went back to the old routine.

Ada was very charitable and generous. Her philosophy was that any charity that comes with some person's name attached was not really charity. Charity was giving to others and not advancing yourself. She came from a non-conventional background. Her family was part of the Seidman and Sons accounting firm in New York City. While she was alive, we never knew and were never told that she created, funded, and supported the Abused Women's Center in Youngstown, Ohio.

My good friend, Irwin Thomases.

Bernita and I were very close to the Thomases and Ada was a severe judge of my social service activities. She tried to teach me to stay away from the glamour of recognition and to address problems realistically. One day, while I was busy interviewing at the Tamarkin Company, I received a call from her to come downtown immediately. She wanted me to join her in a march on city hall. I couldn't get there and that really disappointed her.

Her vital being and her strong moral code of right and wrong were so different from anyone I had ever known. Like my mother and Bernita, Ada Thomases' influence on me continues to this day. Her commitment was so strong and selfless that I continue to emulate her unwavering dedication to causes.

Sadly, Ada developed cancer. One Sunday afternoon when she was very ill and suffering badly, she and Irwin invited Bern and me to come for cocktails. We had champagne, hors d'oeurves, and kibitzed for a while. We left their home that day and never saw her again. Bern and I later realized that it was her goodbye party to us.

Chapter Four

Bernita and I moved to Palm Beach in 1980 and lived at the Sun and Surf condominiums for approximately four years. During that period we had a wonderful social life. My sister Fran and her husband Nate belonged to the Palm Beach Country Club and introduced us to their friends and other club members.

We were admitted to the club, which is one of the two most prestigious Jewish country clubs in the United States; the other is Hillcrest Country Club in Beverly Hills, California. If you are not charitable, as well as honorable, you might as well not apply for membership. If you can afford to play, you can afford to pay. Our family had always been a very large contributor to the Youngstown Jewish Federation, so the requirement of charitable giving was not a great concern to us.

Above is our first home in Palm Beach, the Sun and Surf condominiums. Below is a typical view from inside the units.

After fours years at the Sun and Surf condominium, we began looking for a more permanent place to live. We were getting tired of our "mirrored wonder" that we had purchased as a temporary home. It was time to move on. There were apartments being built across the street that were really beautiful and we kept admiring them. They were expensive and the prices were raised every year, although the units weren't selling. It was ridiculous. We took our time and did nothing. When the builder finally went bankrupt, we purchased the best apartment in their smaller building at one half of the asking price. We were financially secure at the time, things were going very well for us, and for a couple of small town hicks, we were swinging.

42   Bernita and Bud, Becoming a Team

Chapter Five
Bernita's Family

Bernita was born July 14, 1929 to Joseph Ungar and Jenny Weiss Ungar. Both of her parent's families had immigrated to the United States from Hungary. I am not sure when the Weiss family came to the United States, but it was many years before the arrival of the Ungars. Bernita's maternal grandparents, Bernath and Esther Weiss, settled in Pittsburgh, Pennsylvania. They lived in a large home on Murray Avenue in Squirrel Hill.

Bernath was in the liquor business and had strong connections with people in the banking industry. He was a successful businessman who invested in real estate. He had a considerable amount of money and was a real patriarch. In the Jewish tradition it is a common practice to bestow the name of a favored deceased loved one on new family members. After Bernath passed away, three grandchildren were given his first name. Two of his grandsons were given the name Bernard and his granddaughter was given the name Bernita.

Bernita's father, Joseph Unger.

The Weiss family lived well. Bernita always talked about the large staff employed by her widowed grandmother, Esther. Unfortunately, when Esther passed away, the Weiss children fought with each other over money, spent all of their inheritance, and in the end, their father's financial success amounted to nothing.

Joseph Ungar, Bernita's father, came from a very large family in Budapest, Hungary. The family was closely interrelated to another large family named Elder. These families intermarried and their lives were continuously linked with each other, personally and in business. Family and work were the only important things in their lives.

Born in Budapest, Joe was the youngest child born to David and Sali Ungar. When David died, Sali was already older and would not leave the rest of her family in Hungary to come to the United States, where her other children had moved. When Joe was young, Sali sent him to Pennsylvania to live with his older brother, Morris, who had become a successful businessman in McKeesport before moving to Youngstown, Ohio in the 1910s. Joe attended the same high school as my father and graduated. He loved learning and continued to educate himself for the rest of his life. In his spare time, he would always sit and read the dictionary.

Morris was Joe's mentor and counselor. He was a respected banker and the patriarch of the Ungar family. He served on the board of the prestigious Dollar Bank and Trust Company in Youngstown and was also a successful real estate investor. After the stock market crash of 1929, he capitalized on his position with the bank. The Ungars were one of the few local families that had not lost their wealth during the Depression. They were able to purchase bank notes at a discount because of Morris's position at the bank, and because they had the cash available, despite the difficult times.

I believe Joe married Jenny Weiss because of family connections, their common backgrounds as Hungarian descendants, and their families' mutual involvement in the liquor and banking businesses. After they married, Joe and Jenny had two children, Donald and Bernita. Their first child, Donald, later married Rita Schwartz from Detroit and they had three children. Their oldest, Judy, was diagnosed with multiple sclerosis while she was attending Ohio State University. She later married, but died in her early fifties. Donald and Rita's other two children, Ricky and Bobby, became lawyers and live in California. After his wife Rita died, Donald married Shirley Sims and they moved to Windsor, Canada.

After Donald was born, Joe and Jenny had their second child, Bernita. Then tragedy struck. While Joe was checking Jenny out of the hospital, she suffered a massive stroke and died, only seven days after Bernita's birth. This tragic history is important because it helps explain who Bernita was, and how she created and estab-

Chapter Five

lished her own unique personality. When Jenny died, her parents wanted Joe to send the baby to Pittsburgh to be raised by the Weiss family, but Joe would have none of it. With no mother to nurture her, Bernita was raised by nannies and housekeepers the first years of her life.

Several years after Jenny's death, Joe married a beautiful woman named Mazie Goodman, but Mazie had none of the smarts or elegance of Jenny. A few years after they were married, she gave birth to her own daughter, Sandra, who later married Philip Fein from Milwaukee. They had three children, Gail, Steven, and Bobby. According to Bernita, Mazie was not good step-mother material and she never succeeded in developing a good relationship with either her or her brother, Donald.

Then tragedy struck again. Mazie was hit by a car and was seriously injured while crossing the street on her way to Temple Anshe Emeth on Elm Street and Park Avenue. She spent many years in and out of the hospital and had multiple serious operations. She was severely crippled for the rest of her life. Apparently, her bad physical state did not help her relationship with Bernita.

Joe loved Donald and Bernita so much that he showered them with material things to make up for his absence from home and the lack of a good family life. He worked at least seventy hours a week. To say that he spoiled his children would be an understatement. At that time, the Ungar family was wealthy and Donald and Bernita were given no boundaries on their desires, especially Bernita.

Bernita sorely missed not having a mother who would have nurtured her or a father who could spend more quality time with her. Joe was a phenomenal man, but was too busy to continually guide her. In spite of this, or maybe because of this, she established a great amount of street smarts. However, she never applied these smarts to a formal education.

When she was eighteen and a senior, her father almost had to buy her out of high school just to get her a diploma, despite the fact that she was the most popular kid in the class. For Bernita, studying was out of the question. When we attended her 50th high school reunion, the entire class all demanded her attention. We had to eat one course of dinner with her black schoolmates, one with her non-Jewish friends, and one with the Jewish kids.

She was always very much in demand because of her warmth and personality. Everyone loved her.

Joe Ungar's sense of humor was very dry and Bernita inherited this trait from him. One humorous story Bernita hated to hear involved the night of our engagement. Someone asked Joe if he was happy about Bernita's engagement to me and he said, "Well, having a daughter is like having a Christmas tree. The Christmas tree is a very beautiful thing just like a girl is before she is twenty-one (Bernita was twenty-three). However, the tree is not so wonderful after Christmas Day, just like when a girl is over twenty-one. Sometimes you may even have to pay to have them hauled away." Bernita inherited Joe's cynical sense of humor and she loved her father very much.

Joe worked hard and was president of a successful meat-packing business named Ungar Brothers. After Bernita and I were engaged, he brought me down to tour his plant. They slaughtered cattle and hogs, broke down the carcasses, and sold them to the local stores and supermarkets. The Ungar Brothers produced sausage, bacon and other by-products. Joe liked to tell us that the sausage and the lunch meat they produced were made to sell and not to eat. I remember how bloody and inhumane the process was. It was horrifying to observe those animals being killed. I never went back to the killing floor again.

Joe and Mazie Ungar; Pearl and Jack at our wedding.

Chapter Five

The meat-packing business was very successful during World War II, but went into a serious decline after the war ended. The major manufacturers like Swift, Armour, and Hormel were having difficulties making a profit. Their prices began to drop, and companies like the Ungar Brothers couldn't compete and still make a profit.

Joe Ungar didn't understand the changing realities of a suburban post-World War II economy and was convinced that owning real estate was the way to make money in the future. Rather than investing and updating their meat-packing business, he chose to buy property. Joe thought that purchasing successful downtown Youngstown properties in the city he knew and loved would secure his financial future. I remember him telling Bernita and me that he wanted to own all four properties at the intersection of Federal Street and Champion Street, a prime business location.

The family purchased the property, but the downtown stores that had been so successful during the previous decades could not compete with the popularity of the newly emerging suburban shopping centers. Ironically, it was a Youngstown man, Edward DeBartolo, who with another Italian family, the Cafaros, led the suburban shopping center explosion in our section of the country.

As it turned out, downtown Youngstown faltered long before other downtown areas, and even before the local steel mills closed. Sadly, all of the Ungars' real estate investments vanished with the demise of a once successful downtown. The entire area has since been torn down. If Joe had spent the same amount of money purchasing inexpensive property in the suburbs, the Ungars' financial future would have been secured.

Joe was a truly wonderful man. He was one of the most charitable people I have ever known and was a real inspiration to his family and to me. He gave millions of dollars to charity. The Ungar family was an important contributor to Temple Anshe Emeth and other Jewish causes. Joe always said that regardless of what he had left in his life, he would still leave this earth with more money than he came in with. He had a very positive effect on Bernita and me because of the example he set. He was very generous and donated so much of his time and money to various causes. This kind of commitment is one legacy that Bernita and I wish to pass down to our own families.

Chapter Six
Our Life on Ravine Drive with Jon and Jeff

The first five years of our married life, Bernita and I lived on the second floor of an old duplex on Elm Street because there weren't any newer apartments available at the time. There was a delicatessen across the street from our apartment with a flashing neon sign. When I brought Bernita home from our luxurious honeymoon and she saw the light flashing into our bedroom window, she said she couldn't believe the classy way I introduced her to our marriage. From her big house on Fifth Avenue, she said, it was a lousy exchange. Every Saturday, however, our friends would stop by our apartment on their way to the deli and we would have a wonderful impromptu open house. Our friends knew there was always an open invitation to visit our home, especially the single ones.

Bernita and I both loved children, but we knew from the beginning of our marriage that my bout with the mumps would affect my ability to get Bernita pregnant. We tried desperately. We had been married for a few years and all of our friends were having children at that point. It was impossible for Bernita to visit her friends in the hospital who had just given birth. Many silent tears were spilled during those first few years. We went to specialists in Youngstown, Pittsburgh, and in New York City. They all said that although it was possible to conceive, it would not be easy. We would have to just keep trying.

Stanley Engel.

At this point, we were desperate and had a terrible time coming to terms with the situation. Nothing we did was working. I would come home at noon during the right time of the month when Bernita was ovulating, and we tried selective insemination in the obstetrician's office. It was getting so that it became an impossible situation. We couldn't keep on like this, it was destroying us. So, we decided to investigate adoption.

The Jewish Family and Children Services was a legal adoption agency, and they arranged adoptions for couples in the Youngstown area. We were not interested in a private adoption through attorneys or physicians. Our social worker at the agency was Stanley Engel, Executive Director of the Jewish Federation of Youngstown, the parent organization for the Jewish Family and Children Services. Both Bernita and I knew Stanley and his entire family very well. He told us on our first visit that he would be conducting an arm's length investigation. There would be no leeway because we knew him and we agreed.

The process took close to two years. Stanley had many meetings with us together, separately, and then together again. There was no letup. It was very difficult. We would ask him if all of this was necessary and he told us that if we wanted to adopt, then we had to go with the process. He would expect no less from us.

Then, on August 10, 1956, we received a phone call from Stanley. It was just a few days after my 30th birthday. He asked us to come to his office to sign a few more papers, again. We asked him if we could come the next day since we had plans to go to a movie that night. He replied no and said that he was too busy in the morning to see us.

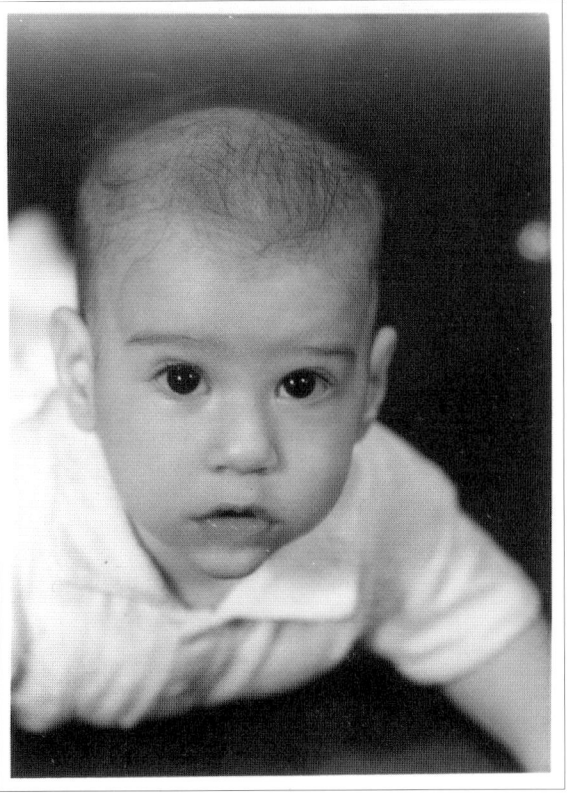

Baby Jon.

When we arrived at his office, we sat down waiting to sign papers, not at all expecting what was about to happen. Stanley looked at us and asked if we wanted to go see our new son, Jonathon David Tamarkin. We were floored! And as I write this down, tears fall, as they have done so many times before. It was the most exciting event in our three and a half years of marriage. After all of our prayers, our son was here.

Stanley took us to see Jon that night and told us that he would be in our home the next morning. With no time to lose, we began our phone calls to get the apartment ready for our baby. We ordered the crib, the bassinet, and all of the paraphernalia one needs. We were friendly with everyone in town, and with the help of family and friends, our mission was easily accomplished by 10:00 a.m. the next morning. Stanley said that we were not

Chapter Six

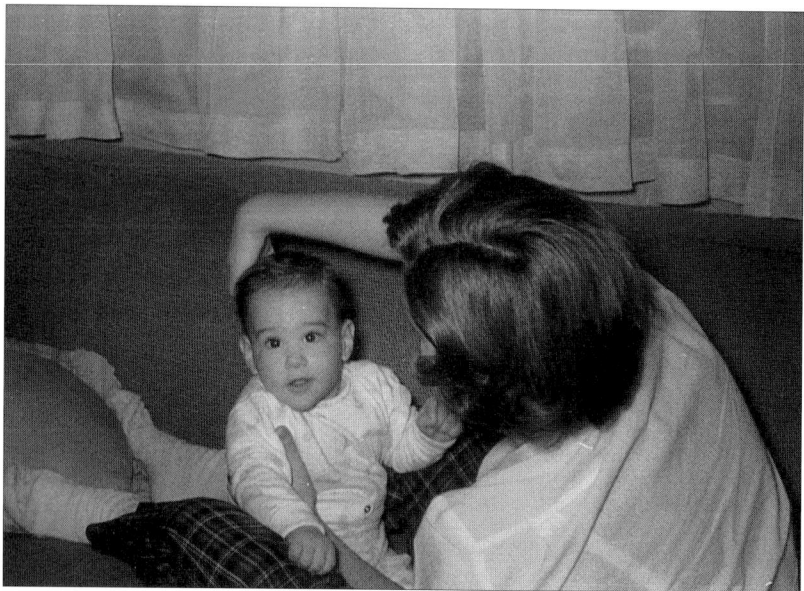

Bernita and Jon.

Grandparents doting on Baby Jon. Joe and Mazie Unger (below) and Jack and Pearl Tamarkin (bottom).

allowed to have a nurse to assist us. He wanted us to take full responsibility of the baby for one week and bond with him. Then, we would be permitted to bring in help.

You cannot imagine our first few days. We didn't know the least thing about raising a little boy, but we learned in a hurry. The presents began piling up and the company kept coming. I smile when I think of the trouble we had feeding him that first day. We didn't know how much Pablum to give him and couldn't understand why he wouldn't eat the amount we had measured. Being thrown into this very new, but thrilling situation was both frightening and exciting. Most of our friends didn't know much more than we did about raising children and we kept receiving too much advice from everyone. We tried to do everything right for the baby and Bernita would have a fit every time he cried. It was a lot of adjusting, but we were so happy that we learned our roles in a hurry. We were permitted to have a nurse the second week, Mrs. Johnson, an older Swedish practical nurse. She straightened us out, trained Bernita and Lilly, our long-term housekeeper, and life became wonderful for our family.

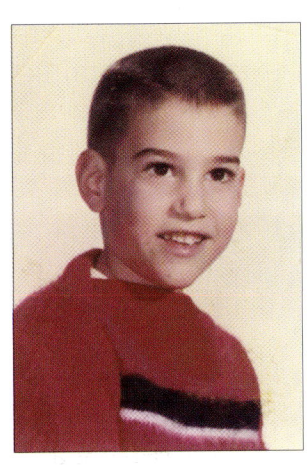
Young Jonny.

Well, as Jonny got a few years older, we realized that we needed a backyard and better living facilities in which to raise a family. It was time to buy a home. We looked around and decided to go to Liberty Township, an older suburb being revitalized nearby. We found a lot on a lovely wooded street named Ravine Drive. There was only one problem; there were no Jewish people living on the street.

The person selling this property was an ex-neighbor and acquaintance from high school, Eldon "Bud" Wright. We also knew his wife, Beverly. He was an aspiring lawyer with the most prestigious and old-guard law firm in town. He knew both of us and liked us. He said that he would be glad to sell us the lot if the neighbors, many of whom were clients of his firm, approved of a Jewish family moving onto the street. He told us he would check with the neighbors and get back to us.

A week later Eldon called me. Only one family objected to us, the Larry Joneses, and Eldon said that since their opinion was meaningless, he would be glad to sell us the property. Naturally, the first people to call on us when we moved in were the Joneses. We became friends with them and with all of our other neighbors. We made a habit of having a party every year for the neighborhood. They were good to us and good to our children. It was a wonderful place to raise a family. Our house could have been a little larger, but I listened to my father and tightened the plans so that we wouldn't have too large a mortgage. Frugality was always the watchword in my father's discussions with me. He trained me well.

Moving to Ravine Drive really changed our lives. We were exposed to people with different backgrounds than our own. A few years after moving into our new neighborhood, the Bill Lyden family purchased a large home directly across the street. They were our age and had five children. Bill's father owned the American Oil franchise in our area and was very successful.

Bill, a Notre Dame graduate, was a big, smart, tough Irishman with quite a wild reputation. Before meeting the Lydens, I learned

Chapter Six

of his reputation one evening when a few of us were dining at the Colonial House, our favorite Saturday night local hangout. Apparently, Bill had just punched someone out at the bar. My friend turned to me and said, "Good luck. That's your new neighbor."

Bernita invited the Lydens for dinner a few months after they moved in. Bill walked into the house, looked at Bernita, and told her that she was that bad girl his mother wouldn't let play in their backyard pool. Well, that began our relationship. Bill remained a bad boy and our very good friend, and was the most wonderful philanthropic bad boy in our community.

Bernita and Donna Lyden became great friends although they lived in different worlds and were completely different in nature. Donna had a great sense of humor and never took herself very seriously. We had wonderful times together. The Lydens got to know our friends because we invited them to all of our parties, and we got to know their friends as well. One Christmas night, we were at their home and they were serving corned beef sandwiches from the Jewish deli. We couldn't believe they were putting butter on their rye sandwich bread, so Bernita and I had to teach those Catholics how to eat corned beef sandwiches.

Bernita was one month older than Donna. When they both turned fifty years old, we had a party for them on our Tamarkin Company warehouse dock. They were born in 1929, so we decided to have a "Depression" party and asked everyone to dress appropriately for that era. We hired a caterer and invited all of the Lydens' friends and all of our friends.

A couple of hundred people attended. We planned a non-fancy party, had portable toilets, and served depression-style food, including shepherd's pie and macaroni and cheese. We had special drinks, and the booze flowed. The party was a great success and we had a very memorable evening. That was our crazy relationship with the Lydens.

Bill and I were so different in nature, and in size, but he respected me and we did great things together. We both worked hard to improve conditions in Youngstown and helped people rally around community issues. He was the ultimate community leader. Unfortunately, the Lydens always had marital problems and they divorced. Donna remarried unsuccessfully. Ironically, when Bill became ill, she became his constant nursemaid until he passed away. When I was in Youngstown a few weeks ago, I had lunch with her and we had a great time reminiscing.

Our life on Ravine Drive was great. We had so many wonderful neighbors. It was a happy part of our lives, raising our families together. After we moved into our new neighborhood, we decided that it was time to have a sibling for Jon. Although we continued our attempts to have a child by natural means, we were not successful. The time had come to see Stanley Engel. Well, we thought, here we go again.

We started the same process as before, had many interviews, and answered many, many questions. "How are you adjusting to parenthood?" "How is your marital relationship?" "Is this going to be a good move to have another person in the family?" It went on and on. At least this time we weren't as nervous. We were confident that we'd be good parents to another child.

Jeffrey as a toddler.

Three and a half years after we adopted Jon, Jeffrey Brian came into our home. He was born January 21, 1959. The adoption process was the same, but the timing was a little different. Jon had been ten weeks old when we received him; Jeffrey was younger and closer to four weeks old. We were so thrilled with the adoption because now our family was complete.

Stanley had asked if we wanted a boy or a girl, and we told him that we didn't care. We only wanted the baby to be healthy. When we were told that it was a boy, Bernita said, "Thank God, I don't know how I could ever raise a little girl."

Jon and Jeff both went to public school. Their growing up was very routine and each boy had his own friends. Jon was more sensitive than Jeff. He was never a rugged child who excelled at sports, so we tried to encourage

Young brothers, Jon and Jeff.

Chapter Six

The boys playing chess together.

Jon (below) and Jeff (bottom).

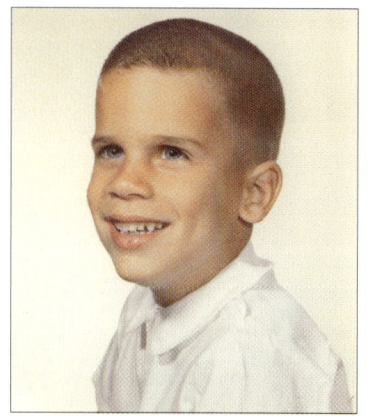

him to do things he enjoyed. Jon was an easy child to raise. He loved the arts and had a great group of friends. He was well-behaved and always tried to do the right thing. When he was thirteen, he had a wonderful bar mitzvah and I took him to New York City to see the World's Fair and the city that I loved. We saw Funny Girl on Broadway with Barbra Streisand. We had a great time together.

By the time Jon reached high school, our public school system was in a deplorable condition. Kids were skipping high school a couple of days a week. Many parents began to send their children to private schools near Cleveland. We wanted our children to develop a full sense of identity, but we didn't want them to commute back and forth every weekend to Youngstown. We felt they should establish a full life somewhere, whether it be at home or away at school.

We searched for a preparatory school for Jon that he would enjoy and that specialized in his interests. We found a Quaker school in Newtown, Pennsylvania, named the George School. He was accepted and did very well there. He finished his education at Colorado College in Colorado Springs, where he received a bachelor of science degree in psychology.

Unlike Jon, Jeff had a very strong and independent personality from the day he was born. He was stubborn and always knew what he wanted. He loved sports and loved to fish every day in a pond on our neighbor's property. He would take empty water pails to our country club, catch fish, and then bring them home to stock his pond. We kept saying that he caught the same fish every day. He loved baseball and football. He played football in junior high school, which distressed his mother endlessly. He played again in high school, but finally gave it up after much prodding to prevent future knee problems. Jeff continued to play baseball throughout his life, however. He currently helps coach his two sons' little league teams.

Jeff despised Hebrew school because it interfered with his sports and after-school activities. It was a real trial to get him bar mitzvahed. We finally had to give him private lessons because he absolutely refused to attend Hebrew school. He was mischievous, as his mother had been. She always said she recognized herself in Jeffrey. One Sunday morning, I spied toilet paper strung across the trees of a neighbor's yard. They were away for the winter and I got very angry and was going to call the police.

Bernita wouldn't allow it and said that she wanted to handle the issue herself. She called Jeffrey to a private meeting and he confessed to the prank. He spent the whole day taking the toilet paper down off the trees, stuffing it his pockets so no one would know what he was doing. Bernita said she knew Jeff had committed the prank because she would have done the same thing at that age. I know I wouldn't have done that; I was probably still dressed in white.

When Jeff reached high school age, we checked preparatory schools for him as well. He chose Hotchkiss, which is located in

An early family portrait (above).

Jon as a young man (left).

Jeff as a young boy (below).

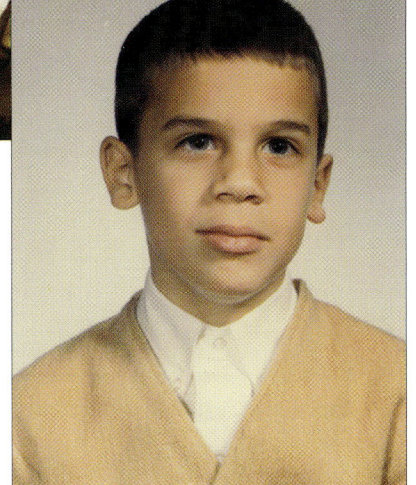

Chapter Six

The Tamarkin family, 1970's.

Lakeville, Connecticut. When we met the football coach at a hotel bar the evening before Jeff's interview, the die was cast. Jeff did very well there and after prep school, he attended Bowdoin College in Brunswick, Maine. He graduated with a bachelor of arts degree in History and Germanic Studies.

Although we were busy raising two boys, we continued to have a wonderful social life. We used the Squaw Creek Country Club extensively while the kids were in school. Bernita played either golf or tennis. She was a wonderful mother. She sent them off to school after a good breakfast and was always home waiting for them when school was over.

Bernita and I realized how blessed we were to have the two greatest gifts of our lives, our two sons. We always loved and adored them unconditionally. They have brought a great purpose to our lives. You two boys, who are now men, have been God's blessing to us.

Jeff fishing with his son Joe on the Intracoastal Waterway, Florida.

The Tamarkin family at Jeff's wedding.

Chapter Seven
Our First Visit to Israel

I can clearly remember the spring of 1948 when the Security Council of the United Nations voted to accept Israel as an independent nation. Listening to each nation announce its vote was suspenseful and emotional for every Jewish person because of their memories of the Holocaust. I think anyone who had access to a radio was listening to that vote being called, nation by nation. Nobody was certain of what the final vote would be, but President Harry Truman backed the resolution that would grant Israel its independent status.

After the Holocaust, the issue of Jewish immigration and the need for a "Jewish Homeland" became paramount. Jewish people throughout the world proclaimed "Never Again!" From the moment the resolution passed, Jewish life changed throughout the world. The Arab nations issued a response to the passing of the resolution, attacked Israel, and the first of many Arab-Israeli wars began.

Funds were raised to support the new Jewish nation and clandestine meetings were held internationally to help supply illegal arms for the settlers. Until that time, no one had ever heard of a Jewish army or Jewish fighters. Because of what happened to the Jewish people during the Holocaust, there was international support for the new nation of Israel. But could a little band of settlers build a new nation and fight the Arab world? It was not a sure thing.

Support from Jewish people all over the world and assistance from other nations and groups made good things happen. The Holocaust was never far from anyone's mind. The Jewish people wanted Israel to become a reality, and it did, due to the resilience of a dedicated band of Jewish settlers and the support of Jewish people abroad.

Every time I visit Israel, I am very moved by the abandoned military vehicles that have been kept as monuments on the road up to Jerusalem. It is hard to believe what Israel has achieved over the past fifty years. As a pacifist, I get upset at times with Israel's

Bernita and I took several trips to Israel. Here I am leading a mission in 1978 (center), accompanied by Jeff and Bernita (to the right of me).

militaristic stance on certain matters. However, I have the softest spot in my heart for everything that it has accomplished. It makes me so very proud to be a Jew.

In 1962, while I held a leadership role with the Youngstown Jewish Federation, Bernita and I, and our friends, Bud and Elaine Spero, were invited to participate in the Second Young Leadership Mission to Israel. It was an honor to be invited. With the support of our families, and the help of our long-term housekeeper, Lil, who agreed to take care of our young children, we left on our mission.

Israel was new and growing, and only a small number of Jewish people from the United States had ever visited. There were forty-five people on our tour, which lasted twenty-five days. Bernita and I had never been to Europe or away from our children for such a long period of time. This was a real experience for us.

When we arrived at New York's Kennedy Airport to depart for our mission, Bernita was very nervous and concerned about being on a plane for so long as it flew over the ocean. She decided to go into the airport lounge where she met another female passenger who was going to drink Scotch. Bernita said she needed two doubles of Scotch, and the other woman suggested that they have three doubles instead. Well, the two of them were a panic, and they had the whole plane in stitches.

Our trip was very exciting. It took place in August and the weather was very hot. When we arrived in Europe, the first stop on our mission was Vienna, Austria. The local newspaper covered our visit and wrote about the young Jews visiting Vienna, an unusual sight since few Jews had visited the area since the days of Hitler.

Wherever we went, people stared at us. Our reason for going to Vienna was to visit refugee camps where families were waiting

Chapter Seven

for passage to Israel by ship. We went to the camps with several interpreters and the refugees talked about their wartime experiences in Poland, Romania, and Russia. Some of them had been in concentration camps and all had stories to tell of how they survived the war. It was a very emotional experience for all of us and we emptied our pockets of everything we had.

Several weeks later, as we were nearing the end of our tour, we saw the same people again when their ship docked in the port of Haifa, Israel. Many kissed the ground when they disembarked. They recognized us and we stayed with them while they waited for their transportation to the immigration centers in Eretz Yisrael (Land of Israel), where they would begin their new lives. It was so very thrilling to be a part of this historic moment in their lives. To witness such events is something you never forget.

During our tour, we visited many settlements and met with many important leaders who spoke to our group, including Ben Gurion, Ariel Sharon, and Golda Meir. Sharon scared me with his aggressive militaristic philosophy. We also visited the homes of many Israeli leaders and gained tremendous knowledge of the problems facing residents of the new nation. It is remarkable what the people of Israel have accomplished in the face of such adversity.

On one part of the tour, we flew to the southern city of Eilat, where the daytime temperature was well over one hundred degrees. Our arrival in the city was scheduled in late afternoon to avoid the severe heat. We stayed in the only hotel there, and ate dinner in a restaurant that was located two levels underground in an effort to evade the heat. With no air conditioning, the government had to offer incentives to get settlers to inhabit the area. Today, Eilat is a famous resort city with many hotels that attracts visitors from all over world.

The resort city of Eilat.

When we departed Eilat, our group embarked on a bus ride to Beersheba. This was about a seven-hour trip with no air conditioning and only a few fans. There were no hotels in Beersheba, so we were all placed with different families locally. The Israelis that Bernita and I stayed with had never met

Americans before and they brought their families and friends over to meet and talk with us.

They were all very curious about America and kept asking us questions, such as How do Americans live? Where do they work? What do they do? Who takes care of your children? Our host's name was Benyamin, which is my Hebrew name. He worked in Dimona, but wouldn't tell us anything about it. I later confirmed that he was involved with the nuclear research facility that had been established there.

During our tour, Bernita and I were able to connect and visit with the family of my grandfather's brother, Nacham, in Tel Aviv. His daughter Rosa Fein invited us and our traveling companions, the Speros, for Shabbat dinner. Although she spoke no English, her young daughter, Naomi, was able to translate for us. We learned that Rosa's husband, a physician, had passed away.

Rosa served us gelfilte fish that was almost black in color. At the time, the food was not very good in Israel, but it was not important because we were very excited about being the first of the Tamarkin family to meet our Israeli cousins. Naomi is now a widow and has two fine sons, Eli and Hagai. Both of them have served in the army and are married with families of their own, living in Tel Aviv. Our family is in close contact with them and sees them frequently.

Bernita was a finicky eater and never did well with foods she was not accustomed to. At the end of our trip, when we arrived at the famous King David Hotel in Jerusalem, Bernita spotted some pastry and got all excited. She rushed to order some, but was quickly disappointed, because it all tasted like paste.

Other points of interest.

Chapter Eight
Selling the Tamarkin Company and the Saga of Phar-Mor

In 1981, Jim Meunice, a banking friend of ours from the Union National Bank of Pittsburgh, came to talk to Nate, Jerry, Jack, and me. He said that Giant Eagle was interested in making an acquisition and that the Tamarkin Company was a prime choice for them.

Giant Eagle was a large and very successful, privately-owned supermarket chain in the Pittsburgh area. We were not really competitors, but had overlapping stores in a few locations. We were told by the banker that there would be no brokerage fees attached to this transaction. Since both companies belonged to TOPCO, a large national supermarket food purchasing group, they knew us personally and trusted us.

We were successful in our business and didn't need to sell. However, our accountants had told us several times that our company was too leveraged. We had borrowed considerable amounts of money to purchase twenty-five supermarkets from national food chains that had left the area when the steel mills closed.

We were doing well with these stores and we were not willing to give up a good business. The accountants advised us, however, that we were getting older and if one of the four partners died, there could be a tax problem; and if two of us passed away, the tax ramifications would destroy us. They had lectured us about these facts for a number of years and advised us to search for more liquidity. Also, when we were approached with this offer, our company was just recovering from a terrible five-week strike by our local teamsters union.

The strike was very difficult for all of us because we had always been a very paternalistic company. My family was wonderful to all of our employees and most of our men had been with us for twenty years or more. My cousin Jack cared deeply for his crew and worked hand in hand with them all the time. He was at the warehouse well before 7:00 a.m. every morning and was always on call in case of problems, personal or otherwise. During the strike, the workers were filled with hatred, calling us all kinds of horrible names. It was so hard for us to believe.

That five week period was a sad time for our family. Although we settled the strike, we were not happy and couldn't believe that our trusted employees had staged such a difficult strike against us. This was the third strike in fourteen years and we took the last one very personally. It was very discouraging. When the offer from Giant Eagle was presented to us after these events, we began to listen.

Several times in the past, companies had made offers to purchase the Tamarkin Company and we never took them seriously. Jack and Jerry were five years younger than I, and ten years younger than Nate. They were not interested in retiring from a successful company at the age of fifty.

It was my understanding that the main reason Giant Eagle wanted to purchase the Tamarkin Company was because of the rapidly declining health of its president, Saul Shapira. Another reason was that they had built a huge automated warehouse in Pittsburgh and needed to increase utilization of the space. Several years earlier, they had started a supermarket operation in the Maryland area, which was not successful and closed. They had all this expanded warehouse capacity that could become a millstone around their neck.

We hired the best mergers and acquisitions law firm in Cleveland; Calfee, Halter, and Company. Our agent was David Carpenter, a partner in the firm. We needed the best, unbiased expertise to help us analyze the proposal. My nephew, Mickey Monus, who had recently joined our company after graduating from college, assisted in the analysis. The firm came back to us a couple of months later with a report. They said if we tightened up some of the particulars of the deal, we couldn't afford to pass it up. It was too good an offer. When the sale was complete, we four partners were given a five-year contract and a limited medical insurance package. It turned out to be a wonderful decision. A year and a half later, our largest local competitor, Golden Dawn Foods, a company with approximately the same value as our Tamarkin Company, sold their company for much less than what we were paid.

After the sale had been completed, Mickey came up with a wonderful idea for the new management team. He found a receptive ear with our new young boss, David Shapira, son of the late Giant Eagle president, Saul Shapira. Mickey had visited the deep-discount drug store called Bernie Schulman's, located seventy miles away in Cleveland. It was a large converted grocery store with a limited

Chapter Eight

selection of very low-priced drugs and sundries, and they were doing a tremendous business. Mickey and David went to visit the store several times and were impressed with the concept. They hired staff with knowledge of Schulman's and began their own discount drug store called Phar-Mor (I guess my family doesn't like to end a word with an "e").

As a member of the "old management" team, the twins and I were not involved in the new Phar-Mor operation, but I assisted with the first grand opening. It was Mickey's show, with the backing of David Shapira. Mickey's father, Nate Monus, was put on the board of the new entity.

The opening of the first store in Youngstown was wonderful. Everyone loved it and business was terrific. Soon Mickey and David Shapira began to open stores locally and then nationally. Everything in the company was peaches and cream. It was so successful that even Sam Walton, founder of Wal-Mart, came to see the stores.

A typical example of Phar-Mor's promotional plan was to rent out videos at an extremely low price. People couldn't understand how they could do it so cheaply. When Mickey was questioned about it, he explained that the people who rented the videos had to come into the store twice; once to rent the video, and then again to return it. He said that it was an inexpensive method of merchandising that brought customers into the store two times.

At its height, Phar-Mor had three hundred stores in thirty-seven states. It had 21,000 employees and was doing three billion dollars worth of business annually. As the company grew, Mickey doubled the size of the former Tamarkin warehouse, but the company still ran out of space. For administration offices, Phar-Mor purchased and renovated the empty six-floor building that once housed the Strouss-Hirshberg department store where my mother had worked. This was the beginning of a revitalization of Youngstown's downtown area. The local community was thrilled. These expansions were expensive, however, and raising money became one of Mickey's biggest responsibilities; but it was also one of his greatest talents.

Talk of Phar-Mor and the Monus family was on everyone's lips in Youngstown. Mickey was considered one of the greatest entre-

Tamarkin-Monus family. Seated from left: Pearl Tamarkin, Jon, Bernita, Jeff, Jack Tamarkin, and Susan Monus; Standing from left: Bud, Nate Monus, Fran Tamarkin-Monus, and Mickey Monus.

preneurs in the county's history. He was honored by everyone. He was a guest speaker at Babson College where he had graduated, and later became chairman of the board at Youngstown State University. The Monus family wielded such influence and power locally that my brother-in-law, Nate, gave the commencement address at Youngstown State University. He received an honorary doctorate although he had never finished his college degree after World War II.

Phar-Mor and the Monuses were flying high. It was strange and wonderful to see all of the new activity that was taking place in our hometown and at our old company location. Some of the Tamarkin Company's former employees, who once held low managerial positions, were now working for Mickey and Phar-Mor, living the high life, building large homes and flying in private planes. My sister

Chapter Eight

Phar-Mor CEO David Shapira (center left) and Phar-Mor President Mickey Monus (center right).

Fran and her husband Nate created a sensation with the way they spent money in such a grand style.

When the company had a private offering of stock, our family was thrilled with the opportunity to invest in Phar-Mor. The stock increased in value and we kept purchasing whenever there was an offering. After the company had been in business a few years, Phar-Mor made a one-time offer to buy back some of the shares. My financial manager advised us to be careful. He believed that in all highly-leveraged investments, it was best to get back your original investment, so Bernita and I sold some shares.

Phar-Mor was not the only source of entrepreneurial activity for Mickey. He and his father, Nate, used their influence to purchase a local beer and wine distributorship. Their new franchise was established with an existing beer distributor whose company was not really thriving. The new company became very successful and generated much cash for the owners.

Mickey and Nate did not invite Jack, Jerry, or me; Nate's Tamarkin Company partners, to participate in this new business venture. We all still continued to work together at the company, however.

During this period of our lives, we had some marvelous times and entertained a lot. One year, with the Monuses, we threw a wonderful "ancestor" party at the country club in Youngstown. Guests had to come to the party dressed as their ancestors.

68 Selling the Tamarkin Company and the Saga of Phar-Mor

Our Ancestors' Party, from Minsk and Pinsk to Palm Beach.

One group of our family and friends rented a horse, some animals, and a push cart, and walked up to the country club dressed in Hasidic Jewish garb. They carried signs that said "Minsk and Pinsk to Palm Beach." It was hilarious.

My nephew Mickey always loved sports. He was a very good golfer and loved to watch sports on television. This led him into another entrepreneurial venture. He decided to start a basketball league for players who were 6' 5" or under. He called his team the Youngstown Pride (Lions) and they played in the Beeghley Center at Youngstown State University. The Youngstown Pride needed teams to play against, so Mickey founded the World Basketball League in several other cities.

Mickey asked me to invest a small amount of money in his new team, which I did, although I knew nothing about basketball. Bernita and I attended all the games and loved the action. At one point, the league had a national playoff in Las Vegas, which we naturally attended and Bernita got to gamble. We enjoyed the entire spectacle surrounding it. The team never did well financially and eventually shut down. A few years after the demise of Phar-Mor, the press revealed that some of the expenses for the Youngstown Pride had been paid for by the Phar-Mor Corporation.

Bernita, Mickey and I always got along famously, but during the height of Phar-Mor's success, Bernita and I lost most of Mickey's

Chapter Eight

attention. He, Fran, and Nate began to move in different circles than we did. Mickey and his first wife, Cindy, divorced and he became engaged to Christa Cannone, a young Italian woman with two small children, whose parents lived across the street from us.

We were all invited to their wedding in Palm Beach, where money was no object. They were married at the Ritz Carlton. Their wedding was attended by all of Mickey's buddies and close business associates. One of their bankers from Palm Beach, Loy Anderson, a notary public, officiated at the ceremony. Christa insisted on wearing the Absolute Vodka gold dress as her wedding attire. It was worth a fortune. Two security men came to Palm Beach to protect the dress from harm. The wedding concluded with Mickey's friends drinking grappa straight up. They convinced Bernita to join them, and man, did she get sick.

Mickey and Christa spent the night on a yacht they had leased from a local resident. The following morning, Bernita and I hosted a brunch for them. When we arrived early to oversee the preparations, we ran into the two security men who had not slept all night. They were in a panic because they didn't know the whereabouts of the gold dress. No one had told them that the dress was going to spend the night on the yacht. The guards kept worrying and asked, "What if the boat sinks?" An hour or so later, Mickey and Christa arrived with the dress stuffed into a small grocery bag. What a sign of the times that was.

Mickey wheeled and dealed on a national level. Probably his biggest entrepreneurial venture was seeking and winning the franchise for the Colorado Rockies, one of the two new expansion teams for the National League in Major League Baseball. Mickey was a great negotiator; and he and his partner, John Antonucci, successfully fought the national power structure through hectic negotiations. After they won the franchise, they enlisted the help of some Denver businessmen to begin the operation. John Antonucci moved to Denver to help manage the team.

Bernita and I were not involved in any of these businesses. However, our son, Jeffrey, who loved baseball more than anything in the world, talked to Mickey about working for the Rockies. Mickey offered him an opportunity in Denver, which he accepted.

By then, Jeff was married to Cathy, who was pregnant with their second child. They lived down the street from us and we were very sad to see them leave our nest.

Many months later on August 2, 1992, our world collapsed. I was sitting at my desk in that six-floor building Mickey renovated in downtown Youngstown, which was filled with Phar-Mor's administrative offices, law offices, restaurants, and other businesses, when my cousin Jack came into my office and sat down. He told me that all the wheels had just come off the whole Phar-Mor empire.

Cathy and Jeff with Jenny and new arrival, Joe.

It was discovered that the Phar-Mor financial success was a fantasy. The company's finances were completely out of balance and there was a duplicate set of books. Apparently, Phar-Mor was not the darling we had all assumed. In fact, the company was bankrupt. When the news broke, the entire Monus clan was attending the Summer Olympics in Spain and was not available for comment. They stayed out of sight for several weeks. It was a horrible time in our lives.

It was at this same time that Bernita and I were planning to move to Palm Beach permanently. The Phar-Mor scandal guaranteed that we would never again return to live in Youngstown, our "River City." From the moment the scandal broke, Bernita and I found it difficult to face the angry local community and couldn't wait to move away.

Mickey had given the city a brief respite from the economic problems associated with the closing of the steel mills. Now, all the dreams of revitalization had gone up in smoke. We were completely dumbfounded about all the things that had seemed wonderful, but were not real. The company's method of operation was against everything that Bernita and I, and the entire Tamarkin family, have ever stood for.

Chapter Eight

The scandal also cost us financially. Our family had established a real estate company named Valu Management and we owned property that housed some of our stores and other investments. Since Nate was the financial manager of the Tamarkin Company, he had assumed the same role with Valu Management.

The four of us were equal partners in the company, but Nate shared his equity with his son Mickey. According to the by-laws of the corporation, each principal was permitted to withdraw a maximum of $100,000 from the company for temporary needs. Nate withdrew substantially more dollars from the company. With all of the Monuses' indebtedness, Nate couldn't possibly repay it back. The twins, Jack and Jerry, and I had to shoulder all the financial responsibilities to which Nate illegally bound us. We also owned many Phar-Mor buildings that were empty. Many of our personal and family investments were sold to pay the bills that were created by the collapse of Phar-Mor. We couldn't sue Nate because he would file for bankruptcy and we would be stuck with his legal fees.

Also, my son Jeffrey had been connected with Mickey in a sporting equipment business that had gone bad. I had to pick up that debt as well because no one else would. That was almost a million dollars. Needless to say, those days were not happy times. We were stunned by the unfolding of events and I felt naïve for believing in all of Mickey's enterprises. I began to prepare an alternative financial plan for my family.

For a while, Bernita and I feared we might go bankrupt through no fault of our own. I called our very close friend and real estate agent, Larry Moens, in Palm Beach, and explained the crisis we were facing. I decided to take a real estate course and work in his office. I then discussed my new plan with Bernita, who became very angry and adamantly vetoed the whole idea. She argued that she would not permit me to change my new life and new career because of my family's follies and excessive ambitions. We managed to pull in our horns, settle down, and pay all of our debts, including all of our charitable obligations. We watched every dime we spent and the only extravagances we kept were our beautiful apartment and our country club membership. We lived close to the belt, realizing that we had to protect our immediate family. Fortunately, two years after the scandal broke, one of our potential liabilities, a real estate investment that had been personally guaranteed by us and Valu Management, became a certainty, and that one large liability became a small asset.

Life for my two sons was also very difficult. When the Colorado Rockies found out that Jeffrey was a first cousin of Mickey Monus, he was discharged immediately. Things became so difficult for him financially that he had to sell the wonderful coin collection he had been carefully trained to collect and had accumulated over his entire life to keep bread on the table for his family.

I spoke with some of my Palm Beach contacts to help him secure a job, and some opportunities were presented, but Jeffrey and Cathy decided to return to Youngstown to be near her family. He then became a stockbroker with a local Youngstown firm, Butler, Wick, and Company, and did well. However, Jeffrey is an extremely independent person and after several years as a stockbroker, he decided to do something on his own. He is now back to his first love, purchasing and selling coins, which he does throughout the Midwest section of the United States. He is very happy.

Jeffrey's wife Cathy had always wanted to be a nurse, but she put off going to school while raising her children. When the children got older, she returned to school and completed her nursing degree. She passed her boards and took a position at St. Elizabeth Hospital in Youngstown where all the senior Tamarkins had been born. I am so very proud of her. She has been a wonderful wife to my son, and a wonderful mother to their three great kids, Jenny, Joe, and Nicky. She is like a daughter to me.

Cathy is a wonderful wife, mother, and daughter-in-law.

When we lost all of our capital, my son Jon said it was one of the most defining moments in his life. He realized that he couldn't keep going in different directions, in different fields, with the help of his parents. He had to set his

Chapter Eight

Jon and Bob on our Alaska Cruise.

Jon with his Academy Award in costume design.

own direction and follow it. He was always attracted to the movie business and had a great sense of style, so he went to work in the costume design industry in Hollywood, California. After several years in that field, he returned to school, received a master's degree in clinical psychology, and is completing an internship as a marriage and family therapist. Jon has been in a wonderful relationship with a fine man named Bob Oppenheimer. Bob is a social worker with Kaiser Permanente in Los Angeles. They have a great life together.

The whole Phar-Mor episode was very painful for me, but even more so for Bernita. She and Fran had been like sisters, even during those years when Fran was spending so much and living the high life. We had always been very close to Fran's and Nate's children, Mickey and Susan; and our children were close to Fran and Nate. Bernita was so hurt and upset that she never lost her anger. The Phar-Mor scandal ended our relationship with the Monus family.

Bernita always claimed that the onset of her cancer was linked to the demise of Phar-Mor. I am not entirely convinced this was true, but her hurt was so deep that it definitely affected her physical state. She was never jealous of the Monus family, but to her, our extended family was sacrosanct. Her father had taught her to trust only her immediate family. She had given that trust to the Monuses and that trust was betrayed. Bernita was never a person to change her position once her mind was made up, and she was so angry that she never talked to any member of the

Monus family again. It was sad to lose faith in a family who had been so close.

Mickey Monus went to trial for his actions. A brilliant Cleveland attorney, James Messerman, was engaged to defend him in federal court. Mickey was scheduled to plea-bargain for a lighter sentence, but at the last minute he told his lawyer that he changed his mind and wanted to stand trial. Messerman was aghast and asked the judge to remove him from the case, but the judge refused. The first trial ended in a hung jury. A few months later, it was alleged that a juror had been influenced. A new trial was held in a federal court in Cleveland. This time the jury found him guilty. The court ordered a maximum sentence.

I was not speaking to the Monuses at the time, so my information is second-hand, but I think Mickey's sentence amounted to eighteen years. He served approximately nine years in a federal penitentiary near Youngstown. The Monus family was destroyed and Fran and Nate suffered greatly. All their high living and high ambitions disappeared. They had to sell their beautiful condominium, give up their extravagant life style, and had to live from hand to mouth in a very modest apartment in Palm Beach with support from their daughter, Susan, a successful real estate agent in California.

There is a sad end to this story. Many years after Mickey was found guilty, my sister Fran was diagnosed with pancreatic cancer and underwent chemotherapy. Sometimes, I would see her at the local cancer center where she and Bernita were both being treated. I always went and talked to her; and when she was hospitalized, I went to see her every day. But I never went to their apartment, that much I couldn't do. When Fran died, I went to the funeral alone, but chose not to go to the house afterwards to be with the family. I had my own problems to deal with.

Fran died a few years before Bernita. When Bernita passed away, I never saw or heard from any of the Monuses except Nate, who attended her funeral. About two years after Bernita's death, I was attending my weekly Saturday foreign film matinee and bumped into the Monuses' housekeeper. She told me that Nate was not allowed to drive anymore. He was suffering from a mild form of dementia. Although I don't have great feelings towards him, it did upset me a bit. It seems that good or bad, we all get older.

Chapter Eight

I also was told that Mickey was being released from prison and planned to move to West Palm Beach with his new wife, Mary. Sometime after he moved to West Palm Beach, I learned that he, Mary, and Nate go to temple every Friday night for Shabbat services. Under the rules of his house arrest, temple was the only place Mickey was permitted to go for several months, in addition to work. Well, I made a feeble excuse to myself and went to temple one Friday night. They saw me and motioned for me to join them. I sat between Mickey and Nate and made my gesture by being there. I had not seen Mickey for fourteen years.

A month later was Rosh Hashanah, the Jewish New Year. Traditionally, Bernita and I had always entertained company for a buffet after temple. We had many friends with no family in Palm Beach, so our lunch was always appreciated. After wrestling with the thought for a few nights, and not considering Bernita's opinion from heaven, I decided to call Nate and invite him, Mary, and Mickey.

Nate sounded confused about the invitation, but said he would try to come. Five minutes later, my phone rang and it was Mickey. He said that while he was in "camp," he had been allowed to use the prison kitchen to cook and prepare kosher foods. His mother, Fran, taught him how to cook the food and corrected his cooking problems while they talked over the phone. He told me that he had already made a Rosh Hashanah meal for his dad and Mary, but asked if was ok for them to come for a drink.

Nate and Mary brought over a sample of all the foods he had made, which included gefilte fish, tzimmas, chopped liver, and goose grievens. It all tasted like my mother's cooking. The food was delicious. During our lunch, I gave a New Year's toast. I told my guests that I hadn't spoken to my family in fourteen years and that the time had come to make peace. I asked all of my guests to think about their own lives and to re-think their histories. It was a new year and time for new beginnings. I knew Bernita was up there somewhere, madder than hell with me for making the gesture, but I can't listen to everything she tells me during our nightly conversations. I am allowed to make my own decisions, sometimes.

The next day I received the following note from my nephew, Mickey. With Mickey's permission, I have included his letter and his poem because the Monus family has been such an important part of my life. With all of his faults, I do like my nephew and hope that the rest of his life can be a good one. He has suffered enough. That doesn't mean, however, that all the problems that my family has suffered because of the Phar-Mor experience can ever be forgotten. They are printed indelibly on my family's hearts and minds. Some hurts can never disappear.

Wednesday, Oct 5, 2005

Uncle Buddy,

    You have no idea what your words meant to my dad (and to Susan and me!) in your toast to the New Year yesterday. I am responsible for the rift in our family because of my failure at Phar-Mor. I can't change what happened but I can apologize to you. Although the story is different and much more complex than the public account, have no doubt, the buck stopped with me. I am so sorry I failed you!!

    I know even more than most how close you and Bernita were and how tough it must be without her. You both were such an integral part of my entire life. My memories go all the way back to your duplex apartment. Be it Friday night dinner at Pearl and Jack's, in Florida, or even Las Vegas (where you went reluctantly) we always had fun together as a family and Bernita always had us laughing! I am sorry for your loss!

    Finally, when I came into the family business, you helped train me and mentor me, making sure that our relationship was not like what Uncle Ben did to you. (I saw it first hand!) I will always be grateful for that. I will never forget what you told me about buying, "if I like the item or product for my own personal consumption--don't buy it for the masses."

    I've enclosed a poem I wrote before I left prison that in many ways sums up my experience.

                                                Love,

                                               Mickey

Chapter Eight

To Finish is to Begin

*You never will know
What true friendships can mean,
'til you've been where I've been
and seen what I've seen;
I've lived in a world
behind four walls
where nobody sees
and nobody calls;
As I look through the windows
at razor wire fences
I dream of the day
when my life thus commences;
I also dream after all these years,
with great anticipation,
my return to my peers.*

*If not for my very special wife Mary,
there is no question I would be contrary;
She visited me three days every week,
even during the times it was so very bleak;
She also said "Yes" when I asked to be her groom,
and we took our wedding vows
within the prison visiting room.*

*Papa, Nanny, Susan
Jason and Brett,
were always there, too,
so I wouldn't fret;
Brett took golf lessons
in visiting room sessions,
while Jason had business lectures
sitting at Elkton for very long measures;
Sister Susan became our family's matriarch,
believe me when I say this is no lark!*

*Papa sent magazines
on a daily basis,
making mail call seem just like an oasis;
Cousin Sam and best friends, Michael and Eunice
just to mention a few
always came to visit
ensuring I never was blue.*

*The internet, flat panel, iPod and eBay,
all came along since I've been away;
Although this is so
please have no doubt
these are the things
I know plenty about.*

*I have in reserve
a backup path,
having worked as a tutor
teaching high school math.*

*My beloved sports teams,
(excluding Ohio State and Coach Tress),
the Indians, Cavaliers, and Browns
are still a mess!*

*To the rest of my true friends
you know who you are,
I will see you all soon
when freed to a car.*

*In my world, to finish is to begin,
I do so now with a very big grin;
You never will know
what true friendships can mean,
'til you've been where I've been
and seen what I've seen.*

– Mickey

Part Two
The Palm Beach Years and Social Advocacy

*Guardian of the Menorah Award,
Youngstown, Ohio.*

The Palm Beach Years and Social Advocacy

Chapter Nine
Creating My Own Identity in Social Advocacy

Early in my career at the Tamarkin Company, I became an active community volunteer. I worked at various local charities and then focused my efforts primarily on our local Jewish Federation in Youngstown. I served on the Federation's board of directors for many years, was chairman of its annual campaign, and eventually became its president. I was very much a hands-on administrator and worked very closely with Stanley Engel, my friend and mentor, who had served as the social worker for the adoptions of our sons.

Chapter Nine

During my presidency, we reconfigured and updated the building that housed both the Jewish Community Center and the Jewish Federation. We built apartments for the elderly with government funds. I oversaw the merging of our federation with the Jewish Federations of Warren, Ohio, and Sharon, Pennsylvania. We also changed the structure of our local Jewish Family and Children's Services. It was really my first experience in creating positive social change. It was a very exciting and I enjoyed every minute of it.

My work with Stanley during these years influenced my approach to charity work for the remainder of my life. We had a wonderful relationship, although we didn't always agree. Every Friday afternoon, he came to my office at the Tamarkin Company and we discussed issues for several hours. At least ten times, he got very angry with me because I disagreed with some of his decisions. Those meetings always ended with Stanley storming out of my office, telling me that his resignation would be in my hands the following day.

He had been with the Federation for at least thirty years and in all that time he never seen a president who was as actively involved in the growth and operation of the agency as I was. Although he would get angry on occasion, I knew he respected my opinions. I admired and honored him for all the lessons he gave me. After leaving the presidency, I continued to meet with him on social service projects until the day he passed away. I respected his judgment immensely and loved him dearly.

Every year I was asked to stay "just one more year," and I did. After nine years as the Federation president, my term finally ended. When I left, I became very involved with the United Way agency in Youngstown and was appointed chairman of their annual campaign. My pitch to local businesses was that the "United Way was the best kept secret in town." No one in the community really understood the wonderful and positive things that the United Way stood for and accomplished. With that slogan, and drawing from my former experience, I ran a very successful campaign, exceeding that year's campaign goal, a first for Youngstown in many years.

While working at the United Way, I met another of my great female mentors, Delores Jennings Crawford. At the time, Dee

Tamarkin says UW campaign seeks to broaden base

Monday
One-on-one
With Bert Tamarkin

Question: When and where will this year's Youngstown Area United Way campaign kickoff be held and what will it feature?

Answer: This year's United Way kickoff is going to be a Party on the Plaza from 4 to 7 p.m. Tuesday at the bandstand on Federal Plaza East.

This year we're having disc jockeys from various radio stations, a hot air balloon in which some people will ascend, and a yo-yo contest.

The Five Sensations, a group of musicians that play '60s and '70s music, will be there. They're young Youngstowners. Everybody likes them. They draw a crowd. They've been at previous Parties on Plaza.

We want this to be an occasion where all our agencies are represented. Our United Way agencies are invited to come down and participate, to bring some of their people to show what they're doing. Some may have booths, some may have T-shirts and other displays.

We're inviting the mayor and the county commissioners and we'd like it to be United Way Day in Youngstown.

If it rains, we'll be able to use the inside of the city parking deck.

Question: How will the campaign strategy this year differ from that of previous years?

Answer: The watchword of this campaign is we must broaden the base. We feel we have to expand the number of companies and people that have been giving donations to us, including those who've never donated before.

Before Black Monday, we received most of our gifts from large industry, especially steel.

Bert Tamarkin is chairman of this year's Youngstown Area United Way campaign, which begins Tuesday.

He retired late last year as vice president of the Tamarkin Co., where he had worked for 39 years, and began to devote more time to his volunteer role in the community.

Tamarkin earned a bachelor's degree from the University of Michigan and a master's degree in gerontology from Youngstown State University.

A United Way volunteer for 15 years, he has served on its needs assessment and executive committees and chaired the 1986 leadership club.

Tamarkin, 61, lives in Liberty Township with his wife, Bernita. They have two grown sons, Jeffrey and John.

The edited interview was conducted by Peter H. Milliken, *Vindicator* staff writer.

Since we can't rely anymore upon large industry, we must broaden our base and get to companies that have never been called upon before. We can raise a lot more money in our community. We have an awful lot of untapped sources for money.

Payroll deduction is a very important part of our campaign, since 60 to 65 percent of our money comes from workers in companies.

For a person who makes up to $15,000 a year, we feel that a fair share gift is six-tenths of a percent of his or her gross annual salary. This means one hour's pay per month. For incomes over $15,000, we feel 1 percent of the annual salary is a proper gift to ask for.

Question: Potential donors are bombarded with solicitations from numerous competing charities and causes. What are the strong points of United Way that make it a wise choice for donors?

Answer: United Way is the only organization in Youngstown that combines the needs of the whole community.

We fund all the organizations of our community that make Youngstown what it is, including the Boy Scouts, Girl Scouts, and Camp Fire. We fund organizations representing all religious sectors, including the Catholic Service League and Jewish Federation.

We cross the religious and economic spectrum. We take care of the poor and the hungry and the whole community.

Out of campaign contributions that we receive here, 98½ cents stays in our community and 89 percent goes directly to our agencies. Only 11 percent goes for administration and fund-raising.

We watch where all the monies are going. We really police the agencies and we make sure that the monies we're raising from people are properly dispensed and that the agencies are using the money properly for services.

We're trying to do away with overlapping services. We feel, in Youngstown, too many organizations have been doing the same thing.

We're trying to spread the dollars that are being raised in this community to where the needs are.

Question: You have a United Way campaign goal this year of $2,750,000. How did you arrive at that figure and by what date do you expect to meet it?

Answer: We met with our agen- (Please turn to page 6, column 1)

Newspaper article about the Youngstown Area United Way campaign.

was the allocations chairman for the agency. She is a very bright African-American woman who came from a large family of modest means. When I finished my term as campaign chairman for the United Way, I began working with Dee as a volunteer on the allocations process. Together, we encouraged and helped many agencies build their effectiveness. We worked with neighborhood groups involved with education, healthcare, and housing. Our purpose was to do more than fund agencies; we wanted to teach them how to work independently and effectively for positive change.

I had no experience working with other ethnic communities; all of my experience was with Jewish people, and Dee would often critique my actions or methods. She taught me ways to change my approach towards different populations and different situations. I learned that some agencies needed extensive handholding and training before they could provide quality service to their communities. It was a great learning experience.

Dee Crawford is a smart, effective leader. Over the years, her reputation grew steadily. When she left the United Way, she took a position with Youngstown State University, and then had a wonderful career as the director of human services for Mahoning County, Ohio. She retired last year. She is one of the special people

Dee Crawford.

Chapter Nine

who has had a permanent effect on my life and with whom I remain in regular contact.

After we had sold the Tamarkin Company, Bernita, who despised cold weather, wanted to move to Florida for the winters and become a "snowbird." I am not a bridge player or a decent golfer, and I knew that I would be bored out of my skull. I have a high metabolism, can't sit still, and can't tolerate inactivity. I had to come up with a plan that would satisfy both of our needs.

I had no desire to start a new business career at this point, but did want to pursue my volunteer work. I liked the idea of a challenge and decided to pursue a master's degree in social work. When I told my mentor Stanley Engel about my plans for the future, he told me that I had to do some rethinking. He said that I already knew as much as the professors about social work, and I would go to class everyday and say "bullshit, bullshit."

Stanley suggested that I seek vocational counseling and find a new direction for my talents. He made an appointment for me at the Jewish Vocational Service in Cleveland, Ohio with the director, Bob Kahane. After a long meeting, Bob set me up with a wonderful counselor who administered a long battery of tests over a few weeks. The test results showed that advocacy would be a wonderful field for me to enter. Before making a decision, however, I was given some very critical advice by the agency director and the test administrator. I was told that advocates cannot expect their names to be in lights, nor can they have an attitude of self-importance. Once programs are established, the social advocate must always take a back seat and then move on to other projects. It is up to the advocate to make other people important. I had been honored on many occasions for my charitable work in Youngstown, so I listened to this advice carefully. I was told that it would not be easy advice to follow, but I knew it would be no problem, and felt up to the challenge.

I enrolled in a graduate program at Youngstown State University when I was fifty-five and pursued a non-traditional degree offered by the Guidance and Counseling Department in the School of Education. I took twenty-five hours of their curriculum, and was permitted to use an outside source for the balance of my degree requirements.

In one class that dealt with non-directive counseling, the students were videotaped as they conducted mock counseling sessions. My first session was a disaster. I was so completely directive in my approach that I was embarrassed to watch myself. I did get somewhat better as the class went on. While my direct approach is probably not the best quality for counseling work, it has definitely been an asset in my social advocacy work.

I remember that I had a terrible time studying for my first final exam. After reading a passage and thinking that I had learned it, I'd go on to the next section. However, I found myself forgetting the details of the material I had read just two hours earlier. I spoke with an advisor about studying at an older age, and was told that when people get older, they learn differently. I began to take notes while studying and this helped me retain the knowledge. I passed my first exam with good grades and then did very well with the rest of my school work. Receiving an additional college degree wasn't necessary, but it helped me establish a discipline and provided some important skills for becoming a knowledgeable and qualified practitioner.

While working on my master's degree at Youngstown, I had not yet decided which population I would like to target. At that time, there were many programs for children in the social service world, but not many for seniors. It seemed to me that the senior Jewish field would probably be rife with advocacy opportunities. With this in mind, I searched for an academic advisor to guide me.

A Jewish gerontology professor from Akron State University was the first advisor I consulted and I worked with him for two sessions, but he was more interested in teaching me about his own field of specialized senior employment than in understanding my ambitions. So I searched for another academic advisor and found Dr. Zev Harel, a Holocaust survivor who had immigrated to Israel and then to the United States. Dr. Harel had fought with the Irgun, the clandestine military organization that operated in the former British Mandate of Palestine. He attended Hebrew University in Jerusalem, Israel, and received a doctorate.

Zev was chairman of the gerontology department at Cleveland State University and established a strong program at the institu-

Chapter Nine

tion. He was tough, very disciplined, and I loved working with him. He taught me everything I would need to know about entering the field of aging. I met with him every few weeks for over a year and did my assignments religiously. After a year of working together, he arranged a special meeting with me. He told me that I couldn't focus my work on Jewish gerontology because my vision was too global. He could see that I was interested in addressing the problems of all people, not just those of the Jewish faith. The work that I had done with Delores Crawford at the United Way had changed my perspective and my life. After this conversation, I went to the Jewish Federation in Youngstown and worked on a project for several days. I realized that Zev was right, my vision had changed and was broader. I would have to reconsider my future goals.

Spending time with our granddaughter Jenny in Youngstown.

While working towards my degree, Bernita and I had already become Florida snowbirds. I had a routine in which I alternated my time between Youngstown and Florida. After I received my degree, we purchased an apartment which served as a temporary residence until we found something more permanent. With my master's degree in hand, I was ready to begin my seasonal work as a social advocate in Palm Beach County.

Cathy, Jeff, and our grandkids vacationing at our condo in Florida.

My work with the Jewish Federation and the United Way in Youngstown afforded me an excellent understanding of the community services that can be provided by a well-run organization. I wanted to establish the same or similar working relationships in Palm Beach County that I had enjoyed in Youngstown. Toward that end, I established early contact with staff and board members of the major funders and service providers in the area, such as the United Way, the Community Chest, the Children's Services Council, the Health Care District, and the Palm Beach County Human Services Department, to name a few.

Since I had no one to pave the way, I made the rounds at the county's public agencies and many of the local social service agencies. During interviews, I explicitly stated that I was not willing to volunteer my services to stamp envelopes, answer the phone, or serve in a mundane capacity. I had a master's degree in the field and was searching for a professional volunteer position. No one took me seriously or understood what I wanted to do. Looking back on it, I don't think I was even sure of what I wanted to do, only what I wouldn't do.

Every agency in Florida has its own unique mission, and I was a one of a kind volunteer. In Florida, we have an overabundance of volunteers looking to relieve boredom on a short-term basis, but I was looking to make a full-time commitment to an undertaking. I wanted to establish my own identity.

I began to volunteer for the Jewish Federation of Palm Beach County and joined a wonderful advocate, Helen Hauben, as co-chair of their committee on aging. Our job was to address the problems of Palm Beach County's expanding senior population. Helen was a wonderful activist who has been very instrumental in establishing the HIPPY (Home Instruction for Parents of Preschool Youngsters) program, which originated in Israel to assist low-income immigrant families. We worked on the aging committee together until the new executive director changed the course of the agency.

I also talked to a couple of state legislators about assisting them in addressing community needs in the county. One state legislator, Lois Frankel, now the mayor of West Palm Beach, asked me to assist her by taking calls in her office and answering questions from her constituency. It wasn't the kind of work that I wanted, but it was a place to hang my hat temporarily.

The following year, I worked with David Demko at Lynn University in Boca Raton, Florida. He was director of their gerontology program. He encouraged me to work with him on an employment program for seniors. Although pleased to be assisting a gerontologist, the work I was doing didn't inspire me. I wanted to be an advocate, but only if I could utilize my own unique skills and stay true to myself and my goals. Up to this point, everyone I was working with was fashioning an identity for me that was not my own. I was very dissatisfied and came to the conclusion that I would rather struggle in the field for a while, and wait for the right opportunity, than give up my goal of creating my own identity and my own future.

Chapter Ten
Meeting the Needs of Our Senior Population

Despite my initial disappointments, my nature is such that I was not going to give up easily on my plans. Discouragement only enhanced my resolve, so I laid out a new plan. Because I had completed a successful graduate internship with the Area Agency on Aging in Youngstown, I offered my assistance to the local chapter in Palm Beach County.

At first, my work with them was very routine and unfulfilling, but then a new director came on board and began to use me for some projects. I was happy to have my talents finally utilized after running from pillar to post for an entire season. I was unaware, however, that the agency was undergoing a state review and investigation regarding issues linked to poor management and inefficiency. As a result, the agency was restructured and set on a new course under the leadership of Becky Gregory, who was program manager for the Florida Division of Aging and Adult Services. She installed a new board and created a new charter. When she called me for an interview, I met with her and she asked what I would like to do for the agency.

Sharing a laugh with Becky Gregory.

Becky has a wonderful story about our first meeting. When I walked into her office for the interview, I was dressed in typical "Palm Beach" attire, including shoes with no socks and colorful clothes. She took one look at me and said to herself, "Well, here comes another dilettante, I wonder how many days he'll last.

I hope that the time it takes to train him will be worth the effort because it looks like I'll have a lot of work with this one!" We laugh about it now because we have become such good friends.

Becky told me that she had a project to investigate and asked if I would be interested in assisting her. The project involved plans that had been drawn up by the former director of the Area Agency on Aging, Robert Moeller, and Rabbi Howard Warshaw, former executive director of the Boca Raton Jewish Federation. They had jointly laid plans for a senior housing project in Boca Raton. Becky asked me to visit Rabbi Warshaw and report back to her on the project's status.

Rabbi Warshaw told me that the Federation was planning to build a housing project that would include both low-income seniors and moderate-income seniors. He believed it would be a wonderful combination of people. I informed him that our grants only supported very low-income seniors, so I could not recommend his project. Understandably, Rabbi Warsaw was not pleased. When I gave my report to Becky, she thanked me for a job well done, and from that day on, she became not only my mentor, but my very good friend. Over the next eighteen years, whenever she changed positions in the county system, she always enlisted my assistance for new projects and challenges.

I was elected to serve as a member of the restructured board of the Area Agency on Aging and served for the maximum period of nine years. During that time, I helped organize their advisory council that represented aging consumers. I still work closely with the agency and they have repeatedly asked me to rejoin the board, but I have found that I serve them better if I just do projects with them. Being a board member is no longer attractive to me. I am more valuable facilitating new projects and then placing those projects in capable hands. I am currently assisting them with two programs, an immunization program for lower-income seniors and a hunger survey of the elderly in Palm Beach County.

Our local Area Agency on Aging represents five counties in Southeast Florida, but over sixty percent of the seniors living within this area are located in Palm Beach County. While serving on the agency's board, I would often propose new projects for Palm Beach County, but the representatives of other counties would

Chapter Ten

then complain that they needed the same projects. I argued that the needs of a large urban area are different than the needs of a rural area. I found their complaints very frustrating. It was a no-win situation. It made me realize that seniors in our county needed their own voice.

As a result, I turned to the United Way for a solution. We consulted with some experts and decided to start our own senior project, the Palm Beach County Partnership for Aging. I have been very active in this organization since its inception. Although I have been rotated off the board this year, I am invited to attend every board meeting and continue to help them with planning. I am the oldest person there; the rest are young practitioners. Come to think of it, I am the oldest person at all of the various meetings I attend.

There are so many things that must be done for seniors who can no longer assist themselves. Increased lifespans are creating serious problems for agencies that aid our elderly population. Aging residents on fixed incomes face insurmountable problems due to high rents, costly prescription drugs, increased insurance rates, and high food costs. For those requiring home health care, it is not uncommon to find long waiting lists for services. The care of our senior population is not up to the standard that it should be. Counties must assume a proactive role because the state and federal governments do not provide sufficient funding.

While volunteering at the Area Agency on Aging, Becky Gregory and I were advised of a new health care initiative in Sarasota which provided medical care for seniors living in poverty. We were told that the program was showing excellent results, so a few of us flew to Sarasota to meet the director and observe the program. We were very impressed. When we returned, I was sent to Dr. James Howell, the director of Palm Beach County's Health and Rehabilitative Services at that time, to discuss the program's implementation in our community.

Dr. Howell liked our idea and suggested that I talk to Dr. Jean Malecki, the new director of the Palm Beach County Health Department. This was the first time I met Dr. Jean. She is a brilliant physician with great vision and is recognized as a national leader in the field of public health. She immediately told me that

Dr. Jean Malecki.

she didn't like the program, but then added that she would like to learn more about me, where I was from and what type of work I did before coming to Florida.

She told me about some of her projects, including her plan to send a medical van called the Med-Mobile to poor neighborhoods. The van would provide mobile medical services to the elderly and disabled residents. She wanted to improve the program and asked me to work with her. Well, that was over sixteen years ago, and I have worked with Dr. Jean and the Palm Beach County Health Department ever since. She permitted me to establish my own role and identity in the Health Department, provided me with my own office, and encouraged me in my efforts to improve community health. We have a wonderful relationship and have always gotten along famously. I am part of the "family," and describe my position there as "Executive Volunteer."

About the same time that the Partnership for Aging was organized, the Planning Association of Palm Beach County was established to coordinate the services of all of the major non-profit agencies in the county. Their board conducted a comprehensive

Chapter Ten

study and found that in too many cases there were duplication of services and also serious gaps in some of the services provided. The non-profit agencies in the county were asked to redirect some of their operations, but it seemed that everyone loved to "talk the talk," but no one wanted to "walk the walk." Each agency tried to protect its own turf and was not willing to make the changes needed. Sadly, the Planning Association's mission was not accomplished.

The board of directors voted to cease operations and split the treasury into two halves, an Alpha and an Omega. The Alpha would fund children's programs and the Omega would fund elderly services. I was a member of the Omega group. A few of our members wanted to fund another study of our seniors. When I heard of the plan to repeat the same type of study, I met with my boss, Dr. Malecki, and we agreed that a repetitious study was not going to solve any of our local aging problems.

Instead, we decided to create innovative programs that would serve as models for addressing the needs of the senior population. Jean and I contacted Margaret Lynn Duggar, a businesswoman from Tallahassee, Florida, who had been the director of the Florida Department on Aging under the administrations of former governors Bob Martinez and Lawton Chiles before beginning her own consulting business on issues relating to aging. I had met her on several occasions and was impressed by her knowledge and her ability to get things done.

She loved the idea of establishing new programs for our seniors and wanted to serve as our consultant. We were delighted because she had many national contacts. We brought together leaders of our local foundations and senior projects, and we hired Margaret Lynn to get the programs organized. She secured three years of funding from both the Hartford Foundation of New York City and the Research Foundation, a national entity which supported innovative senior programs. It was a very exciting and creative time for our committee.

A local lawyer, Kerry Rodriguez, was hired to lead the project. In addition to the grants we received, another primary source of funding was the Quantum Foundation of West Palm Beach. We did a tremendous amount of work with Quantum's Jeanette

Meet A Mensch

BERT "BUD" TAMARKIN

Biography:
Lives in Palm Beach, married to Bernita. The couple has two sons and three grandsons. Formerly of Youngstown, Ohio, where he was in the supermarket business. He's lived here for 18 years – nine years as a snowbird and nine years full-time.

After retirement, Tamarkin obtained a master's degree in advocacy from Youngstown State University's School of Education and was intent on using his new skills to serve in the social services arena. (He received an undergraduate degree from the University of Michigan.) Tamarkin works full-time as an "executive volunteer" for the Palm Beach Department of Health under the leadership of Dr. Jean Malecki, the health department's director.

Community service:
Using his business background and his advocacy training skills, Tamarkin participates in the area of social planning and community initiatives for the health department. Among the projects he's involved in is the establishment of a countywide Hunger Coalition.

Tamarkin also serves on the steering committee of the Omega Project, a long-range project to promote independent living for seniors, and has helped initiate a project for children that strives to "to place a nurse in every school in the county." He also serves on a committee to place social workers in elementary schools.

Motivation to volunteer:
"I love the work I do," Tamarkin said, adding that he's always been involved in community services, serving on executive boards of the United Way and Partnership for Aging.

"I put on a shirt and tie and come to work every day. I have my own desk, my own computer."

Playing golf, he says, was not enough of a challenging retirement for him. "If you played golf the way I do, you too would look for something else to do," he said with a laugh. ▽

– Bea Lewis

Bud Tamarkin is working to improve the health of Palm Beach County.

Corbett and Tim Henderson. The foundation was a key player in the Omega project and provided office space and wonderful support for us.

Omega worked jointly with the State of Florida and the administration of Palm Beach County making it easier for seniors to apply for and receive needed services. With physicians and hospitals, we also established programs that facilitated searches for individuals' specific needs. A big part of the program consisted of helping seniors obtain prescription drugs at reasonable costs.

Omega set up a senior diabetic telecommunications program with our local Health Department and the Area Agency on Aging, which linked frail senior diabetics with nurses and nutritionists. We supplied the group's participants with home computers and taught them how to monitor their medical readings at home. The results from this group were compared with a group that was not involved in the program and we were able to test the efficiency of our project. We also worked with fire rescue personnel and nursing professionals in outreach locations to provide flu shots to impoverished seniors throughout the county who had not been served previously. The immunization program is still very successful.

Unfortunately, after our national funding was withdrawn, Omega was never able to sustain the big breakthrough that we desired. We were unable to continue the program's services. I felt terrible about it. The Omega program was my baby and I couldn't succeed in making it a permanent part of our county's services. It was a major disappointment. The program had so much potential. But I have learned that you can't win them all and you have to be satisfied with what you can accomplish.

Meet a Mensch article in the "Jewish News."

Chapter Eleven
Assisting People with Disabilities

Becky Gregory and I teamed up once again after she joined the Florida Division of Vocational Rehabilitation, an agency that provides training and vocational rehabilitation to people with disabilities. She found that there was a great need to create an entity in Palm Beach County that would give people with disabilities a stronger voice and representation in community affairs.

Becky and I were able to join forces with several local advocates who supported the independent living movement. The goal of this movement was to establish independent living centers that would provide community support services to the disabled population. With this support, individuals could choose to live independently and have more control over their lives. The centers are generally run by those with disabilities and disability advocates.

Two very active advocates, Donna and David Batelaan, helped us lay the foundation for our project. They both use wheelchairs and run a mobility equipment distributorship in Lake Worth. Another very active participant was Bruce Karr. He is a retiree who uses a wheelchair and runs a tennis program in which the ball is permitted to bounce twice. To see these games being played is very exciting.

Donna, Dave, Bruce and many other dedicated people worked hard to establish the new entity. The result was the creation of the Coalition for Independent Living Options (CILO). We worked closely with the Palm Beach Habilitation Center in Lake Worth and we successfully established the agency.

When Bernita and I went to New York the same year that CILO was organized, I investigated several organizations dedicated to assisting disabled clients. One agency that I visited so impressed me that I have never forgotten it. It was the Center for Independence of the Disabled, New York. Its director was an extremely disabled woman who needed to breathe air continuously through a tube attached to her wheelchair, but her handicap did not hinder her at all.

She was really a tough and wonderful advocate. She fought the establishment, knew everyone, and provided housing and arranged services for disabled people. I was fascinated by her and her agency, and returned to Florida anxious to establish similar projects here.

Soon after that trip, I received a phone call from Becky. She said that the time had come to let CILO develop and grow without our involvement. They had an established board, a mission and a staff, and our active support was no longer needed. She pointed out that although it was hard to let go of this project, it was necessary so that the new agency could grow on its own. Well, I was disappointed, and that finished my work in the field of handicapped services. I learned my place in the scheme of things. Over the years, I have now learned when to start and when to walk away from a project.

Becky has been a dominant figure in my Palm Beach life for many years. Her moral standards are of the highest order. She is extremely bright and taught me to expect positive outcomes for the work we do. We have been a wonderful team. Becky is now retired, and she and her husband are moving to North Carolina. That does not stop our calls about projects, however. We will never lose contact with each other; she serves as my conscience.

My friend, Becky Gregory.

Chapter Twelve
Public Health, Education, and Advocacy

Several years after I started working with the Health Department, Jeanette Freeman Hartzell was hired as Executive Director of Volunteer Services. She created an efficient and organized volunteer services division. Jeanette and I are wonderful friends, and serve as sounding boards for one another. My office at the Health Department is next to hers, and we communicate freely and create many projects together.

Jeanette Freeman Hartzell.

Over the years, I have served with the Health Department on many projects. When Lawton Chiles established the Governor's Council for Community Health Partnerships, he chose the Palm Beach County Health Department to implement the initiative in our area. The goals of the initiative were to develop effective agreements between the public and private sectors to deliver more efficient services to the public. When Jeannette joined the Health Department, she expanded the program. To this day, the Governor's Council serves as the basis for much of the work that I do in the community.

The Governor's Council assists Palm Beach County's Community Action Council and Human Services Division in providing a vehicle for funding of summer camp scholarships to children from low-income families. This is done through the Summer Camp Scholarship Program. In 2006, we sent over two thousand children to day camps. We hope to increase that number in the future and also to improve the quality of the camps. These camps provide structure and activities for children of working families.

Our council has been involved in a multitude of projects, including a dental sealant program for elementary school students, and a foster grandparent program that connects senior volunteers with children in head-start programs. We also provide immunization programs for both children and seniors, and during the holiday season, we coordinate food and toy distribution programs. We are very proud of what the Governor's Council has accomplished since its inception.

My work with the Health Department has been very rewarding. One success that I am particularly proud of is the re-establishment of the school nurse program in Palm Beach County public schools. The former program had been discontinued many years earlier due to a lack of funding. Nursing functions were then assumed by the school office staff. A new source of potential funding became available with the creation of the Health Care District of Palm Beach County, a non-profit public agency funded by local real estate taxes. Its mission was to provide uninsured, low-income residents, including children, with access to healthcare coverage.

Dr. Jean Malecki serves on the Health Care District's board of commissioners. Providing proper healthcare for our student population had always been one of her key missions. We knew the time had come to address the lack of nursing coverage in the public schools. I was assigned to work with Tim Henderson and Randy Palo, both employees of the Health Care District at the time. We put together a plan that would insure a strong program.

We worked cooperatively with the Quantum Foundation and hired a national consultant to analyze the issue of funding and of implementing the new school nurse initiative. Our committee included advisors from local charitable foundations, major social service agencies, the county's board of commissioners, and the school district. We had a great advocate with Ron Armstrong, the school district's Director of Student Services, who also served on our Governor's Council board. Ron provided continuous help and made great things happen despite the hurdles we encountered. In the end, we secured funding from multiple sources and established a new school nurse program that operates under the auspices of the Heath Care District. This project is the envy of all of the other school districts in Florida.

The consultant we hired for the program, Anne St. Germaine, warned us, however, that a preventive mental healthcare program was almost as important as a school nurse program. We were

Chapter Twelve

advised that while state services were available for severely troubled students, none was available for the overly quiet child, the one who could develop serious problems in the future. We came up with a program proposal, but it was not approved. The costs were too prohibitive. We accepted the decision, but knew the issue needed to be addressed in the future.

A few years later when the killings at Columbine High School in Colorado occurred, our committee reconvened. That tragedy was a perfect example of why overly quiet children, often from middle-class families, should not be casually overlooked. The Columbine incident provided the momentum to institute a preventative mental healthcare program in some of our elementary schools.

I served on the steering committee that provided assistance for developing the plan. My role was to meet with the principals, get their approvals, and work with them until the program was established. We concentrated primarily on kindergarten and first-grade students whose behaviors indicated that they might need extra support. We started in fifteen schools and over the years the program has expanded to forty-seven elementary schools.

The professionals we employed held master's degrees in social work or had equivalent experience in the field. Their titles were Behavioral Health Professionals (BHPs). A young clinical psychologist, Dr. Seth Bernstein, was hired to manage the program. Seth and I have developed a wonderful working and personal relationship, and he has become like a third son to me.

Seth Bernstein.

While I was introducing the nursing and mental healthcare programs in the county's elementary schools, I met Delorisa Brown, principal of Barton Elementary. The school is located in a low-income area of Lantana. Principal Brown, who was born and raised in that area, is a dedicated educator who continuously works for positive change in her neighborhood. She is a hands-on administrator and the two of us have become big buddies.

Our first project together began six years ago. After I presented the preventative mental healthcare program to her staff, she asked to have a meeting with me. She explained that her school was having problems passing the yearly FCAT (Florida Comprehensive Assessment Test). Many of Barton's students came from families with little or no education, and many were immigrants who lived in poverty-stricken neighborhoods.

Delorisa Brown, a dedicated educator, in front of the architectural drawing for the new Barton Elementary School.

She explained that some of the children were entering kindergarten without knowing the alphabet, and some didn't even know their last names. They didn't know how to stand in line, how to pay attention or behave in class, or even how to play with other children. The children's lack of academic readiness was a problem because it held back the progress of her entire school; and Principal Brown would not accept a low grade.

Delorisa believed that if she could teach her pre-kindergarten students social and behavioral skills, and provide pre-reading and pre-math instruction, then the testing results and educational progress of her kindergarten class, and of the entire school, would improve. She was so committed and so persuasive that I went to seek assistance from my friends, Tana Ebbole, my mentor and executive director of the Children's Services Council; and Nate Nichols, her wonderful deputy director.

The Children's Services Council is a second county taxing district agency that funds programs for underserved children. Tana is a brilliant woman and true community leader. Because of her vision and efforts, some wonderful opportunities for needy children in Palm Beach County have been created. Nate is an innovative, intelligent executive who works in tandem with Tana.

Chapter Twelve

My friends and mentors, Nate Nichols and Tana Ebbole of the Children's Services Council.

He and I have become very good friends and work together on many community projects. Both Tana and Nate provide constant support for my interests and goals. At this stage of my life, I don't have a tremendous amount of patience and they put up with my constant attempts to find more timely solutions to community problems.

Tana was very interested in the pre-kindergarten program and we set out to create a model program at Barton Elementary with the assistance of other community preschool professionals. During the first year of the Summer Pre-K Enrichment Program we enrolled over one hundred students in five classrooms. We had one teacher for every ten children. The program was a complete success. The next year, Debbie Labella was hired to oversee its expansion. From the first day, Debbie and I became a team and have worked together constantly and beautifully. We are so close that I feel like a real member of her family.

Over the next four years, we expanded the project to cover thirty-two more elementary schools. Approximately six thousand children were provided with the socialization and academic skills they needed for success in kindergarten. The program also assessed the vision, hearing, and educational needs of these school children and provided them with glasses and hearing aids. We worked with special needs children and were instrumental in placing them in special education programs early. Last year, we were pleased to have been honored for our work. Because of the work of Principal Brown and others, the overall grade at Barton Elementary has

Celebrating the success of the Summer Pre-K Enrichment Program.

102 Public Health, Education, and Advocacy

been raised to an "A," which is a phenomenal success. It was very exciting to be part of creating a program that so positively influenced many young lives.

The long-term results of the pre-kindergarten program confirm that we are not teaching our children early enough. Quality learning must begin in the first three years of life. The Children's Services Council believes that one of our greatest challenges as a society is to change the way children are reared and educated during these first years. The council is dedicated to very early intervention especially in the poorest and most underserved areas in Palm Beach County. I am very proud to be asked to work with the Children's Services Council in establishing this important initiative.

This past year, another issue came up at Barton Elementary. An immigrant parent approached Principal Brown and said that she wanted to learn how to read and write English. If she could learn the language, she could have a much fuller life and be able to help her children with their schoolwork. She had taken some evening English classes, but the instructional emphasis was on filling out applications and forms, rather than on reading and writing.

Principal Brown came up with a wonderful idea. Since the funding for teacher assistants had been cut a few years earlier, the teachers at Barton Elementary were very much in need of some classroom help, particularly in the primary grades. After consulting with a first grade teacher, Delores informed the parent that if she collected papers and volunteered in the classroom, she could sit with the class and learn how to read and write. Five or six months later, this mother was able to write her first letter in English, which she sent to her husband and her parents back in her homeland. She was so pleased that Delores cried, the woman cried, and I cried. This was our inspiration to develop the program further and create a Parent University.

The Children's Services Council provided funding again and Mary Washington, a very qualified teacher employed by the Literacy Coalition, was hired to teach the immigrant parents to read and to write English. In return, the parents had to commit a certain amount of volunteer time to the school. Mary felt that she could handle an enrollment of ten parents per class, but on the first morning of class, fifteen parents showed up. Mary needed an assistant,

Thank you letters from the students at Barton Elementary.

Chapter Twelve

so yours truly took the job. What an experience it was for me to be a teaching assistant, often with a two-year-old on my lap while helping with the class. It was a priceless experience.

At the end of the course, we took our adult students on a field trip to the local science museum. While these parents did learn some English, and a few found jobs, the two and a half hours a week that we provided were not sufficient for language fluency. Because the need is so great, we are currently restructuring the program in order to make a greater impact.

Parent University at Barton (above and below).

As I continue to work in the fields of public health and early childhood education, I am increasingly convinced that much more needs to be done to improve the quality of public education. Our children deserve this. My work in these fields has given me the opportunity to observe the complex problems that arise in educating children who come from such diverse ethnic backgrounds, with different spoken languages and unique family situations. We need much more parental and community involvement if we are to insure the future success of our citizens. In Palm Beach County, we have a rare opportunity to initiate effective changes because of our progressive local structure that is supported by the Children's Services Council, the Health Care District, a receptive school district, and other wonderful foundations that focus on positive outcomes.

My relationship with Seth Bernstein has enabled me to become involved in several other school projects. A few years ago, Seth asked if I would help him with the development of some academic and social programs at the newly-built Pleasant City Elementary School. Pleasant City is an area in close proximity to downtown West Palm Beach. Its residents live in extreme poverty and the neighborhood has become ravaged by drugs and hopelessness. Teenage pregnancies and drug addictions are all too common, and too many children are raised by single parents or by grandparents. I have a history of working in this area for over eighteen years.

Many years ago, when I first joined the Health Department, we provided some medical services to this area once a month through the use of our Med-Mobile. At that time, however, it was very difficult to convince the population to avail themselves of our free services. Very few people ever came to the van voluntarily.

We had implemented the medical van program with the help of Gloria Williams, the long-time director of the Pleasant City Community Center. During this period, she asked me to serve on their community center advisory committee and I agreed. We worked very hard to create positive change and we helped established an additional facility with innovative programs. Sadly, no real or lasting changes occurred. I served on this committee for several years, but I found myself working aimlessly and withdrew from the project.

Seth's request for my help with his programs at the Pleasant City Elementary School presented a fresh challenge and I hoped for a better outcome now that the new school was completed. For years, the area's young children were bussed out of their community to all ends of the county because of state racial integration policies. The children spent almost two hours a day being transported to and from school. They had no time to participate in after-school activities or work with school staff. When the new school was completed, students no longer needed to be bussed. They were now within walking distance of their school and Seth wanted to create programs that would help these deprived children attain success. His plans gave me the momentum to return to the area and work for positive results.

Unfortunately, parental involvement was basically non-existent. From the beginning, only a few parents would attend meetings. We asked the mayor of West Palm Beach, Lois Frankel, to provide staff

Chapter Twelve

support for our parental recruitment efforts and she helped us create a committee of community planners. Despite our efforts, it was difficult to get the community sufficiently involved.

Part of the problem was cultural apathy, which is very difficult to change once it has been established in a community. Despite all of our hard work and the work of a fine principal, Andrea Peppers, the school remained a "D" school. Today, we are having some success thanks to the tough and dynamic new principal, Jacqueline Perkins, but there is still a great need for educational support in Pleasant City. Jacqueline has wonderful ideas and I have new hopes for the students and families of Pleasant City Elementary.

During the past two years, a good part of my education work has been centered on assisting residents in the town of Pahokee, which is located forty-five miles west of Palm Beach, on the shore of Lake Okeechobee. It is a truly poverty-stricken area that has been devastated by two serious hurricanes over the past few years. Many people have lost their trailer homes to these storms and have become homeless. The local supermarket was so severely damaged that it closed for two years. Families were forced to buy necessities from smaller stores that charged exorbitant prices.

The future of this community seems hopeless unless the population is educated to break the cycle of poverty. My mission is to work with Palm Beach County agencies, the school system, faith-based organizations, and local industries, to help lift up the people of Pahokee and provide them with opportunities to achieve a better standard of living for themselves and a good future for their children.

The school system is providing extra programming and educational resources to help the children of Pahokee learn to read and write on a higher level. We are extending the hours that the school is open to offer students additional education and assistance with their homework or other needs. Also, we are focusing on improving teacher training and adding incentives to help more teachers become certified. I am continually working to assist in this area. I work closely with a young woman from the area, Cornesha Dukes Chisholm, and also with the staff at the Beacon Center and the Glades Initiative. Our tasks are very challenging, but possible with community support and cooperation.

With all my involvement in the Palm Beach County schools, it became clear to me that I needed a higher level of contact within the school system if I were to get things done. Not being shy, I made an appointment to see Ann Killets, the school district's chief academic officer. We met and she liked my ideas.

Interacting with our preschool children.

Ann is very bright and is able to institute changes. She works long hours and gets up much before dawn. When I found out that she was an early riser like me, I became her 5:30 a.m. caller. She is a delight to work with and a tireless advocate who is interested in making positive things happen for our students. Ann also helped direct me in ways to utilize the "Special Opportunity Fund" that Bernita and I created with the contributions we received from our 50th wedding anniversary celebration. She put me in touch with Jody Gleason from the Education Foundation who helped us establish a web page that provides resources for our high school students to find opportunities for advanced placement in colleges and universities. The program has been very successful and I hope to improve it in the near future.

My second line of support in the school district's administration is Judy Klinek, Director of Supplemental Educational Services. She assists me greatly in my planning and projects. She tells me where to go and what to do to gets things accomplished. I love the things we have done together. Judy is also an early riser and I usually talk to her around 6:15 a.m.

One final education success story I'd like to share involves Palm Beach Public, an elementary school on the island of Palm Beach. The majority of the school's students are children of recent Hispanic

Chapter Twelve

Palm Beach Public's outstanding strings program.

immigrants and they are bussed to the school from areas near Palm Beach.

Approximately eight years ago, Louise Grant, who manages the Pew Educational Foundation, informed me that funding to continue the preschool program at Palm Beach Public had been partially approved. Louise added, however, that the Pew Foundation directors insisted that half of the funding for the program be provided by the residents of Palm Beach. The purpose of the program was to provide immigrant children with language instruction so they'd be proficient in English by the time they entered kindergarten.

I contacted the Palm Beach Community Chest and we discussed the issue. A meeting was set up with potential donors and we were able to raise the money in record time. Beth Walton, the newly appointed director of the Community Chest, became my wonderful new cohort. We have done some great projects together. Her office is located in my apartment building so we have developed a strong relationship. If I don't show up in her office for a week, she wants to know where I have been.

Beth and I then organized the Academic Excellence Committee for Palm Beach Public, which was originally chaired by Edie Schur, but is now run by Ellen Sussman. Our committee is a very effective voice for the school. We established a successful tutoring program staffed by local Palm Beach volunteers. We support a very exciting strings program that now attracts students from all parts of the county. The program is run by a wonderful musician, Andy Matzkow. His three orchestras, which include children with disabilities, are a wonder to behold. He has over one hundred fifty children involved. You can't watch this program without shedding a tear and feeling a burst of pride.

Our committee remains very committed to the success of this school. The school's rating, which was initially low, is now an "A." We have established a gifted program and now some local students are enrolling in the school. We have high hopes for the future.

My ambition is to make Palm Beach Public a model for the entire county. It demonstrates what can be done when quality education is provided to all children, not just those who can afford private schools. I feel that I haven't been able to convince enough people of the important link between public education and the future of our country. We are throwing away a great opportunity. What worries me is that I am eighty years old and may not have enough time to finish all the work that still needs to be done.

Chapter Thirteen
The Hunger Coalition & The Community Food Alliance

A serious issue has surfaced during my work in public health: hunger and obesity. Hunger is a major health problem in our county and the unmet nutritional needs of different populations often lead to obesity. Hunger issues are not exclusive to the unemployed. We now know that too many people in Palm Beach County, even working two jobs, do not earn enough money to adequately feed their families nutritious food.

Train the Trainer seminars offer training to teach residents how to prepare nutritious meals.

When Becky Gregory became director of Palm Beach County's Division of Human Services, she asked me to join her and a few others in finding a solution to the county's hunger needs. Included in this group were community activists, agency representatives, and at times, local business people. The group named itself the Hunger Coalition, and right from the beginning, we decided that the coalition would have only one agenda—to end hunger in Palm Beach County.

We had all experienced the frustrations associated with a bureaucratic infrastructure, so we agreed that there would be no staff,

Observing a Train the Trainer seminar.

no budget, just dedicated people addressing the issue of hunger. Our rules were simple. We would only discuss and act upon those issues that pertained directly to the coalition's agenda, not anyone's personal agenda. One of our first initiatives was to institute a program that would provide lunches to school children during summer vacation. During the regular school year, well over 50,000 children receive free or reduced-fee school lunches, so our big concern was, "What do these children eat during the summer?"

The coalition secured approval to open meal sites at various schools and locations throughout the county. We then printed and distributed a circular which showed residents where the meal sites were and when they were open. We have grown from 18 sites ten years ago to 172 sites this past year. My work with the Hunger Coalition has been the highlight of my advocacy work in Palm Beach County. It is the only advocacy group that has ever been able to stay completely focused and on task.

Approximately four years ago, Becky Gregory persuaded the Hunger Coalition to undertake a food security survey of our county, utilizing the United States Department of Agriculture's Food Security Survey Module for our task. The purpose of this survey was to analyze food intake in areas where family income was approximately $35,000 per year. Our job was to determine if these families were "food secure," or getting enough nutritious food to eat on a regular basis.

Becky enlisted the help of Terry Bozarth, the retired director of Adopt-a-Family. They raised $140,000 from various public and private sources to fund the project. The United Way also agreed to serve as our financial agent and contribute towards the project. Palm Beach Atlantic University offered a group of students to conduct house-to-house surveys and Dr. Jean Malecki of the Health Department secured gratis statistical analysis from Dr. Robert Duncan and the University of Miami.

The results of the surveys were frightening. Of all the nationwide surveys that had been taken using this module, the residents of Palm Beach County were found to be one of the most "food insecure." The statistical analysis showed that eighteen percent of Palm Beach County families earning approximately $35,000 per year ate less than they needed to maintain a healthy lifestyle, and the adults in these families sometimes reduced the size of their meals or skipped meals. We found that over nine percent of our county's children had skipped meals in the last three or four months. The hunger among these children is three times the national average for the same income levels.

A meeting of the Community Food Alliance Access Committee led by Pat McNamara.

These figures were alarming enough to call a meeting of numerous local agencies and begin a community-wide effort. The result was the establishment of the Palm Beach County Community Food Alliance, a volunteer

Chapter Thirteen

organization that examines and addresses the issue of hunger. This organization is a challenge, but also a great joy and demands much of my attention. I don't serve as an officer on the board; rather I serve as a facilitator, insuring that things get done.

I was interviewed about our food alliance by Kelley Dunn, a local NBC news co-anchor, for her program "Kelley's Heroes." The work we do is so important that a full-time administrator is being hired to direct the program.

The Community Food Alliance works closely with the SHARE (Self

Discussing hunger with NBC News Anchor Kelley Dunn.

Some of our junior volunteers.

Help and Resource Exchange) food program. SHARE is a national food cooperative that purchases and delivers quality food, including fresh meats and produce, to central sites throughout the country. Recipients pay a very reduced price for high quality food packages and in return they are asked to donate two volunteer hours per month. The food that arrives at the central sites is picked up and distributed by local agencies, churches and community centers. The food needs refrigeration, however, while it is being distributed, especially to areas far from the central site of delivery. To better serve citizens in these areas, our alliance raised funds and purchased a refrigerated truck to deliver the fresh food.

The Community Food Alliance's role in the SHARE program is to increase the number of sites that distribute food and increase the amount of food reaching families. Before we became involved in the program, churches and community groups were driving to Miami to pick up the food. Now, the local Goodwill Industries warehouse serves as our local distribution point and agencies pick up their food and distribute it once a month through their own volunteer programs.

Today, there are thirty-seven distribution sites. We have succeeded in our efforts because of dedicated people such as Tracey Lamport, who ran the food security survey; Cindy Bartosek, Community Health Director for the Health Department; and Nate Nichols, Deputy Chairman of the Children's Services Council. Cindy and Nate are co-chairpersons of the initiative. I am so proud of what we have accomplished that I often take groups of people on tours to see how the

Food being distributed to hungry families.

Chapter Thirteen

Dedicated community members led by Ian Oudit (right) who runs the Gleaning Project.

Pat and Ana McNamara set a wonderful example for their children.

food is delivered and received by hundreds of families in need. I am always sure to show them the wonderful work done by advocates Dan Shorter and his wife, Jacquie. I am honored to have them as my friends. The services that they and their church provide cannot be overestimated. I love the SHARE program because it is based on the principle of people helping themselves.

The Community Food Alliance also established "gleaning" projects that take volunteers from our area to the fields of western Palm Beach County to pick fresh produce that was not harvested; and if unpicked, would otherwise go to waste. This is done with the permission of some wonderful farmers. The produce that is collected is distributed to local food pantries that then deliver it to families in need. Providing nutritious produce to these families reduces food insecurity and hunger. This past year, I went out with one gleaning team to the corn fields. That was quite an experience for this eighty-year old body, but I had a blast doing it and plan to do it again.

Gleaning corn with my friend and fellow advocate, Nate Nichols.

Ian gives us our gleaning instructions.

Tough, but rewarding work.

Chapter Fourteen
Being a Social Advocate

I am blessed in that I have had both the means and the abilities to enjoy a long twenty-year career in volunteer services with numerous Palm Beach County agencies. I work as an independent entity, control my own activity; and in this way, I am able to place my talents where they can best be utilized. I'd like to think that I have achieved a reputation as someone who works for the common good and seeks to improve the health and education of all of our county's residents. Being a social advocate is never accepting the status quo.

My greatest passion is to examine community problems and enlist the assistance of qualified people and agencies that can help solve the problems. I work with others cooperatively to launch programs that will improve lives. I am not a charity provider. My goal is to help individuals to help themselves.

My work with the United Way provides a good example of how I approach social advocacy. I became involved with the United Way through Tenna Wiles, a wonderful social advocate who was the vice-president of the United Way of Palm Beach County and now serves as executive director of the Palm Beach County Medical Society. With her encouragement, I began working with some of the agency's aging programs and was then invited to join the board. I was introduced to Scott Badesch, a strong leader and current executive director of the United Way of Palm Beach County.

After a couple of years on the board, Scott appointed me chairman of the Community Initiatives Committee and I served in that position for two years. During that time, I organized a culturally diverse group of community leaders to better assess how my committee and the United Way could help them improve services throughout the county.

I never was one to accept existing situations that I knew could be remedied. At every United Way board meeting, and if the discussion was pertinent, I brought up the needs of the county's underserved populations, even if those needs were at odds with the United Way's position on the subject. I remember one occasion when the agency's ex-president and one of its leaders pulled me aside and asked if I realized that I was working outside the parameters of the United Way. I told him that my mission was not to serve an agency, but to serve the people who were the most in need. I served on the United Way's board for over nine years and continue to serve on two of the agency's most important impact areas committees. In 2004, I received their "Volunteer of the Year" award.

I continually look for ways to improve my effectiveness. Early on in my advocacy career, I learned to seek out key people, agencies, and foundations that could analyze problems and help me accomplish my goals. Utilizing programs that are already tested, proven, and run by good leadership is of prime importance. A program is only as good as the people who actually administer the activities.

When new programs are established, it is not necessary to "reinvent the wheel." With the all of the available information on the Internet, social advocates can easily conduct research and take advantage of programs that already work. I find that too often agencies repeat old policies that have not worked in the past. Too many agencies, intentionally or not, protect their own turf so completely that their abilities to fulfill their missions are compromised. Agencies must be flexible and able to adapt to our dynamic and highly technical world. We must all work together, not in competition. As Becky Gregory reminds us, "We all have to learn to play in the sandbox together" if we are to efficiently serve our residents.

Social advocates must learn that their role as facilitators is to serve and improve the quality of life of others. They must put aside their own prejudices. A social advocate has an opportunity to make a significant difference in the lives of individuals and in the community as a whole. A career in the social service field is not always easy, and is not highly compensated, but it is tremendously rewarding.

Becky and Buddy "playing in the sandbox together."

Part Three
Losing Bernita

Losing Bernita

Chapter Fifteen
Fighting a Courageous Battle

About fourteen years ago, Bernita began having pain in her legs. We went to our doctor several times, but he didn't do anything to find the cause of her pain and looked at her condition very casually. We then went to see a well-known chiropractor in town, but the help he gave was very temporary. We needed a better solution.

I had become very friendly and played golf with an orthopedic surgeon named Bob Green. Whenever Bobby saw Bernita, he expressed concern about the way she

Chapter Fifteen
Fighting a Courageous Battle

walked. One night he saw us at a dinner and talked to us about it again. He said that he was going to schedule her for a series of x-rays.

Soon after she took the tests, Bob referred her to a local oncologist that we knew, Dr. Neil Rothschild. Neal was very kind and had a wonderful beside manner. He diagnosed Bernita with multiple myeloma, which is a cancer of the blood cells inside the bones. It causes bones to break. There is no cure for this type of cancer.

We were told that the life expectancy for someone with multiple myeloma was approximately six years, depending on the progression of the cancer. We were shocked and stunned. Bernita was only sixty-two years old at the time and we were just lifting our heads above water after the Phar-Mor fiasco. How could this happen to us now? What do we do?

We believed what Dr. Rothschild told us and took his suggestions, but we also felt it was important to seek out the best authority in the country on this disease. After much investigating together, we learned that Dr. Robert Kyle, of the Mayo Clinic in Rochester, Minnesota, was the leading authority on this type of cancer. Dr. Rothschild spoke with him several times, and Dr. Kyle agreed to take Bernita as a patient.

Naturally, Bernita was very frightened about the illness, but being a realist, she knew she had to follow doctors' orders. She was determined, however, to live as normal a life as possible. We didn't know it at the time, but Bernita was very fortunate in that her multiple myeloma was very slow growing, and she was able to play golf for several years after her diagnosis.

We went to see Dr. Kyle at the Mayo Clinic once a year in Minnesota when the snow got off the ground. It was an excellent hospital, but it was organized like a factory. You took a number and waited a turn for every test given. Although the waiting was hard, every test was done with the greatest care. Robert Kyle was wonderful to us, as was the entire staff at the hospital. He was always ready to discuss new methods of treatment or provide answers to our questions. He worked closely with Dr. Rothschild, our Palm Beach oncologist, and Bernita's care was wonderful.

One possible treatment for multiple myeloma was a bone marrow transplant. Both of Bernita's doctors, however, did not believe she would be a good candidate for this procedure. Then, eight years after Bernita became sick, researchers discovered that the old but dangerous medication, Thalidomide, relieved many of the symptoms associated with myeloma and contributed to successful cancer remissions. During the late 1950s, Thalidomide had been prescribed to pregnant women to treat morning sickness and as an aid for sleeping, but it was taken off the market decades ago after it had been found to cause birth defects.

Bernita's doctors prescribed it for her, but she hated it, and could not take more than one pill per night. We had to fill out forms and a waiver every month just to purchase the medicine. One of the forms was an affidavit that made me swear to use condoms every time Bernita and I had sex so she wouldn't get pregnant. Of course, we laughed about this because of our past reproductive history, and that Bernita was in her late sixties. The whole thing was ludicrous. Thank God, we were able to still laugh at ourselves despite her physical condition.

When Bob Kyle retired from active practice, we were advised to seek out Dr. Ken Anderson at the Dana Farber Cancer Institute in Boston, Massachusetts. He was doing wonderful things for multiple myeloma patients. Neil Rothschild was concerned that Anderson's new methods and drugs might be too experimental and dangerous, but after further consultation, we were assured that Anderson would know how to handle Bernita's case.

Dr. Anderson was a joy. He was a very young man, very warm and friendly, who didn't take himself seriously. We loved him. He was accomplished in his field and later became very well-known, testifying before a U.S. Senate subcommittee on multiple myeloma with patients and spokespersons Geraldine Ferarro and Mel Stottlemyre. We were fortunate to have his assistance during this time.

About eleven years after she was diagnosed, and after a wonderful period of relative stability, it became obvious that Bernita was losing ground and that the disease was progressing. A few of her best friends began gathering around her to assist in any way possible. Her very good friend, Audrey Goodman, would not give up on her and was a constant companion, as were her friends Lita Fromstein, Barbara Levinson, and Barbara Stern.

Chapter Fifteen

Bernita's 75th Birthday Party. Standing from left: Barbara Stern, Audrey Goodman, Lita Fromstein, and Mindy Coker, Bernita's beautician and friend. Seated from left: Barbara Levinson, Bernita, Lorraine Friedman.

This was in the beginning of 2004. Bernita's seventy-fifth birthday was in July of that year. Her friends realized that Bernita might not survive until July, so they planned an early birthday party for her in April. They sent out a notice to all of her friends at our country club announcing the party. The response was phenomenal. Over one hundred forty women came to celebrate Bernita's birthday. She was frail, but so thrilled that day that she talked about it for the next month.

Wonderful speeches were made by many of her friends, and Helaine Allen presented her with this Academy Award speech:

Good Evening,
(It was afternoon)

Close your eyes and pretend that you are at a great celebration. It is a great honor to announce the award for the following category. The nominations for best female comedienne are:

Ellen DeGeneres – for her stand-up performances and comedy show.

Rosie O'Donnell – for her derisive and sardonic humor and ability to capture large audiences.

Joan Rivers – for her witty fashion interpretations that add much to Oscar Night.

Bernita Tamarkin – for her quick wit, a natural comedienne, a situational humorist, a brilliant commentator with her tongue-in-cheek observations of the human spirit.

And the winner is…

Guess who won that award? Bernita never gave up hope even for one day. When she reached the point that she was truly suffering, and it was obvious that she had little quality time left, Neal and I had a meeting, and he told me it was time to stop treatments. With the pain she was having, giving her more medical treatments to keep her alive another month seemed wrong. When we told Bernita that we were going to stop the treatments, she strongly objected, and asked if there were something else we could do. She was very unhappy, but she understood her condition and together we had all planned for this eventuality.

Neal told me to call Hospice of Palm Beach County and ask for assistance. I knew their chief medical officer, Dr. Gail Cooney, and asked her to come to our home and talk to Bernita. Bernita wanted none of it, and although she signed the papers, she wouldn't let Hospice get near her. Instead, we hired our own nurses and Bernita hated all of them. The only person she wanted was our wonderful housekeeper, Barbara Dainty, who had been with us for

Our housekeeper and friend, Barbara Dainty.

Chapter Fifteen

twenty years. So Bernita, Barbara, and I made a deal. Barbara would stay with Bernita for ten to twelve hours a day. I would take over for four to six hours and then I would supervise the nurse for the next eight hours. That wasn't what Bernita wanted, but it was the best I could do for my stubborn Hungarian princess.

Bernita was in bed for several weeks. The end was near, but I didn't realize it. I wasn't being realistic because I was too emotionally involved to see that she was declining day to day. I thought it was a temporary situation. I now regret that I didn't send for our children earlier. One night, Bernita was suffering terribly and Barbara and I tried to help her, but we couldn't handle her by ourselves anymore. We called Neal and he told me to give her a tranquilizer, but I didn't have anything stronger than aspirin in the house. We never took medicines. He called in a prescription and I went to the drugstore and got something to settle her down.

He advised me to call Hospice that night, which I did. They sent someone over early the next morning. The social worker couldn't have been nicer. We decided to put Bernita in Hospice to get her medicines straightened out and then we would bring her back home. I truly believed that was our purpose for admitting her. When the hospice medics came a few hours later with a stretcher, Bernita looked at me with those piercing eyes, as if to say, "I'll get even with you for this!"

When we got to the Hospice center that morning, Barbara told me that she would stay with Bernita during the daytime and that I should

Bernita and Charles Bronfman.

stay with her at night. This way if Bernita woke up, she would see one of us and not be frightened. I agreed and stayed with her each night. When my friend, Charles Bronfman, found out that we were at Hospice, he spent the entire next day with me.

Charles and Andy Bronfman on our visit to Israel.

Even at that time, I was not facing the inevitable. The medical staff told me that they would adjust Bernita's medication and we could go home in a couple of days. I was not thinking realistically, and no one told me anything different. I sincerely believed that they were just getting Bernita back in shape and we would be going home again.

Two mornings later, when I thought she was improving, a social worker asked me where Bernita was going to be buried. "What did you just say?" I replied. I couldn't believe what I was hearing. Bernita was nearing the end and I was in my own world and had made no plans.

I immediately called for the kids to come to Florida and started to make burial plans. I went to see Rabbi Howard Shapiro, and discussed my wishes. I wanted a memorial service in Palm Beach with our friends and our children, followed by a short abbreviated one day shiva (memorial) at our home. Then I wanted to take Bernita and our children back to Youngstown for the burial. It was not the normal routine, but the rabbi agreed to my plans.

The temple was filled with our friends, and many of the people I work with in social service. I gave the eulogy because I felt that no one knew Bernita like I did. She was a different kind of cat and only I had the knowledge to really talk about her. The following is the eulogy I gave for her.

Chapter Fifteen

Celebration of Bernita

Anyone who knew Bernita Tamarkin knew that she was a one-of-a-kind model. She was truly unique. She may not have been an intellectual, but she was certainly smarter and more intuitive than most of the intelligentsia. She had more street smarts than anyone I have ever known. With her tremendous sense of humor, and unrelenting drive, she established in herself a strong sense of identity. She knew who she was, and she knew what she wanted. She always abided by her strong principles, and would accept no less from herself or from anyone else. She made friends with all kinds of people who loved her and remembered her. She had a wonderful, generous heart that she shared with people from all walks of life. She was not only a legend, but a truly great lady.

Bernita and I were married fifty-one years. We were a great team. We always had fun together wherever we went. We had different personalities. I was a so-called intellectual, and she was the comedian. Our similarities were that we were both extroverts and we both loved people. Our moral and ethical standards were identical and unwavering.

Our 50th Wedding Anniversary.

Her support enabled me to become the person I am today. Her encouragement allowed me to establish a new direction in my life. For that I will be eternally grateful. Everyone knows that we did everything together. She was my best friend. When she was still able to play golf, and we played together, people would tell me that I hit the ball almost as far as she did.

Today, my family and I want to give thanks, and celebrate the people who helped Bernita during this last very difficult year of her life. I cannot begin to name names, but those who really helped her know who you are. We do thank you.

For those who participated in her pre-75th birthday party, you should know that this gave her the greatest pleasure of this year, and for those who showed her that respect, you have my family's gratitude.

In a different light, we celebrate all the efforts of the staff of the Cancer Institute, our other medical friends, and Hospice. You were all very considerate of us, and became our good friends and constant companions.

I want to give a special thanks to our wonderful housekeeper, Barbara Dainty. Barbara established a new role for herself and was Bernita's main support system and her best friend.

However, the greatest celebration of Bernita's and my life are our two sons, Jon and Jeff, who Bernita particularly nurtured and loved more than anything in her entire life. They truly have been the greatest joy to both of us and helped establish a purpose in our life.

My Bernita.

I'll first introduce my younger son, Jeffrey, from Youngstown, Ohio, husband to Cathy and father to Jenny, Joe, and Nicky. He will be followed by our older son, Jon, from Los Angeles, who is here with his partner Bob.

Chapter Fifteen

Team Tamarkin at our 50th Wedding Anniversary celebration.

Our boys spoke beautifully. Jeff spoke with a sense of sorrow, but tried to temper it with his mother's sense of humor. Jon, our sensitive son, really broke everyone's heart when he spoke of the loss of his mother. There wasn't a dry eye in the house.

We ended the day at our condominium. We had a spread that Bernita would have planned. Our friend, Andy Bronfman, planned and took care of the whole affair. She literally took it over, including washing the dishes after supper. We flew to Youngstown the next day. Friends gathered and we spent the entire day with Bernita's old buddies, telling stories. We certainly had lots to tell and lots to laugh about. There were so many Bernita stories. She would have loved every minute of it.

Well, life without Bernita began. Our housekeeper, Barbara, informed me the next day that she would be working for me until the day I died. That was her promise to my wife. Without Bernita around, the phone didn't ring and all the action stopped. Her friends said that since Bern was no longer their source of information, they didn't know what was going on in town anymore.

Bernita and I had many serious conversations during the last year of her life. We talked about what I would do with our beautiful oceanview apartment after she passed away. Although I hung on to it when our finances took a nosedive after the Phar-Mor incident, it was too big and too expensive for one person to maintain, and Bernita knew I was going to sell it.

Before she died, she told me that I was a cheap-assed bastard, and if I were left to my own devices, I would live like a hermit, and squirrel away my money. She said that she would haunt me unless I lived well. And I believe that is true, because she still talks to me most nights, and we discuss things. She also told me that I could really become a star because I could drive at night, but that I had to be very careful. Bernita and I felt that it was our responsibility to insure that our family would be taken care of after we were gone, and that our grandchildren would have access to the best education available.

We loved our oceanview apartment in Palm Beach.

Bern warned me not to get caught up with "very high living." We often quoted her father, Joe, who always said that "It wasn't the high cost of living that hurt; it was the cost of 'high living.'" She said we didn't live that way as a couple and I couldn't afford to do it as a widower. She kidded me about remarrying, but I think that deep in her heart, she knew me better. I hope that she is proud of the way I am leading my life today.

The sadness of losing Bernita did not disappear in the months following her death. After a year of mourning, it was time to set the stone over her grave in accordance with Jewish tradition. My family ordered a tombstone with a special inscription. Bernita had not been religious, but her heritage was very important to her. After many weeks of discussion and thought, we came up with the following inscription. It wasn't religious, but it was all Bernita:

BERNITA UNGAR TAMARKIN
July 14, 1929 to April 13, 2004

A VERY SPECIAL LADY

**LOVED BY EVERYONE,
ESPECIALLY HER FAMILY**

Chapter Fifteen

    We all decided to have a private unveiling at the cemetery with just our immediate family, no clergy and no friends. Everyone in the family, including our three grandchildren, agreed to write something about what Bernita meant to them personally. We then had a celebration, the way she would have wanted, with the champagne she loved and her favorite hors d'oeurves, hot dogs wrapped in dough.

    At the party celebrating her life, we read our tributes, drank our champagne, and toasted Bernita. It was a memorable afternoon. A piece of all of us was left at the cemetery that day, but as Bernita always liked to say, "This too shall pass." Here are the tributes from each of us on that special day.

Ode to Bernita
by Bud

*The reason for today's celebration
is to show how Bernita affected the
life of each member of our family.
It is not really very difficult for me
to analyze what Bernita Ungar
did for me and how
she changed me to be
the person that I am today.
She accomplished it over a long period.
I was married to her for fifty-one years,
which is two-thirds of my life.
The friends who know me
understand that she was my wife
and she was my life.*

*Yes, I am a new person because of
Bernita's influence and encouragement.
Since she passed away
my life has some obvious emptiness
because I am doing this alone, and don't
have anyone to share these things with.
However, I am not lonely.
I have many friends,
and I go out too much.
My best friends are the people I work with.
I see them every day
and they give me wonderful support.
I have many people in my social life
with whom I am very friendly.
I keep myself extremely busy
and will do so as long as I have a
clear mind and adequate health.
I love the life I lead
and I am not willing
to make any changes to it.
Remaining single and continuing my work
is the way I hope to spend the rest of my life.
I am not searching for a companion.
If some wonderful person would appear
that would make my life better
without sacrificing my principles,
I would be receptive.*

*However, when I see the world
from my current perspective,
I am convinced that I have already had the best,
and don't know about the rest.*

Chapter Fifteen

Jon

Mom,

I know you're in heaven watching over us
I see you laughing at the things we do
that strike you as funny
I feel you're still with us.
Your big heart and big personality
Full of life, full of verve
Making fun, having fun, and being funny
Telling stories, making people laugh,
giving people joy
Always with a bright optimistic attitude
Buoyant, vivid, strong and declarative
In the morning saying, "It's a beautiful day"
And it always was a beautiful day
growing up on Ravine Drive.
Life was full of love
Full of beauty and hope and energy
Your strong spirit burns bright
Your lifeforce, the thing that made you.
When I think of you now
I think of Ravine Drive mostly,
getting up in the morning
and living a wonderful life
with a wonderful Mom
A Mom with a heart as big as the universe,
bright and colorful, full of sunshine.
You lived your life with dignity and character
and taught me by your actions and attitudes
I feel blessed to have been your son.
We are blessed to be your family
If there's one thing I've learned from you
it's to live life with dignity and humor.

Jeff

For me, Mom meant being a character,
doing something good with life,
having a strong command of dignity,
and much more...
she was, and is, unforgettable.
She brightened up thousands of lives.
No one who met her initially
didn't catch her warmth and humor.
Those who crossed her suffered her wrath.

Mom meant being a crumb picker-upper,
a lint picker, someone who always said
"This too shall pass" and
"would you like another?"
this or that fifty times, give or take twenty.

I remember Mom's stories.
The butt contusions, how she had the
first convertible in Youngstown,
and promptly rear-ended some old fart.
How she was kicked out of Ferry Hall Prep School...
but not why. Never why. I asked a lot "Why?"
She always refused to tell me why.

Mom on skis. Not for long.
She was Lucille Ball and Charley Chaplin
without balance, panicking to stay out of the snow.

Hitting a line drive at my weak backhand,
after I hit her at the net, and snickering away.
Mom was not going to let anyone off easy.

Except at the Northside Bowling Lanes,
when mom left her keys in the ignition.
Guess what happened?
And we watched, not many days later,
as a tow truck went past Anshe Emeth
with the carcass of Mom's car attached.

Mom in the bathtub after my wedding,
naked and drowning, telling Dad as he pulled her up,
"Save the necklace! Save my necklace!"
That was Queen Bernita following the wedding.
There is no reference to the
Royal Magyars having a queen,
but there is no doubt
of the savoir-faire surrounding Mom.

She knew almost everything about
everyone who mattered.
Her pose showed a poise of dignified air.
Maybe she should have been a politician.
She didn't forget a face or a name.

Chapter Fifteen

*Given her honesty and knowledge
of right and wrong,
Mom would have been a great president.*

*No offense Dad, but Mom did rule our family.
It was in her looks more than her words.
Her eyes and her mouth seemed to say,
"You will do this," when she wasn't speaking.*

*I'll never forget in 1965 or '66,
Mom slapped my face so hard my neck almost snapped...
and I deserved it after breaking someone's
windshield with a snowball.*

*Mom put up with most crap, but when her
maid almost burned down the house,
or came to work bloodied
after an accident, she wasn't too thrilled.*

We won't mention Phar-Mor...

*Mom never wanted to give up.
Mom hated quitting.
She was the opposite of a quitter.*

*Many images flash in my mind.
Her taking me to the doctor's for shots,
her attempt at fly-fishing,
her hitting the golf ball at Squaw Creek,
low and hard, long and straight.
We would call it a "Bernita Shot."
Mom in the stands when I played baseball,
and especially football,
making sure her baby wasn't hurt.*

*Mom approaching Willie Mays
in Detroit, "Hi, Willie."
The beaming face of Mrs. Douglas MacArthur,
after Bernita recognized her.
"Thank you so much dear, for talking to me.
It has been so long since someone noticed me."
Mom would never let anyone
or anything to go unnoticed.*

*Maybe I didn't love you enough, Mom.
Maybe you loved me, and us, too much.
I regret being mean, shouting at you,
taking you for granted on too many occasions.*

*I don't regret loving you then, and now,
and I will always cherish the great memories of you.*

Cathy

I knew I liked Bernita the first time I met her.
What I didn't know at that point was that
she would end up being an important
part of my life and that I would love her.
She was funny, people-smart,
kind, committed, and courageous.

Her favorite line of advice she would give me
when we talked on the phone was,
"This too shall pass."
I am happy to say that she was right.
Now I find myself repeating,
"This too shall pass,"
and I smile after those words.

I could go on and on
but what stands out in my heart
and my mind is that she loved me
and she loved our kids with all she had.

It was and still is an honor to
have shared almost twenty years
with such an exceptional woman.
We celebrate her life
with every story we hear,
and every thought that passes,
every day.

Chapter Fifteen

Jenny (age 14)

*Nanny and I were very alike.
The first thing that comes to mind
when I think about Nanny
is her strong opinions.
She stood up for what
she believed in and did not let what
people thought about it affect her.
In many ways, I am the exactly the same.*

*Also, Nanny was very social.
She had many friends and it was easy
to see that everyone loved her.
I respected and looked up to her
very much for this,
and hope to someday have as many friends
and people who love me as she did.
She was fun, a great person, and
understood me like not many people do.
She always stuck up for me
when I begged to go shopping.
She would say to my Dad,
"She'll kill you with her shopping,
but she's a girl!"
She felt where I was coming from.
I enjoyed spending time with her
and we had great conversations.
Most kids today think of their grandmother
as somebody who is out of style and
out of touch with the modern world.
I can honestly say that I had a hip grandma
who loved me just as much as I loved her
and who taught me so much about the
kind of person I'd like to grow into.
I miss her and love her a lot
but believe that she lived
her life to the fullest
and should be remembered
not only for her strong will,
but for the impact she had on
so many lives, including mine.*

Joe (age 12)

Nanny was a really good grandma.
She meant a lot to me.
Nanny taught me to always
strive for my goals and
not to worry about the little things.

Although I did not get to see her much,
whenever I was around,
Nanny always made me laugh.
She was a really funny person.

I never got a chance to see Nanny golf,
but I heard from many people
she was an excellent golfer.

Nanny was really smart too.
Whenever I had a problem,
I knew I would go to her.

Nanny was a great person and
she helped me and a lot of other people.
I loved her very much and I still do.
I will never forget my Nanny.

Chapter Fifteen

Nick (age 8)

*Nanny was a great person
and I loved her very much.
And one of my best memories
is at my sixth birthday party
at "Animal Trails," and
she was scared to go on the wagon,
but she did it for me.
But when she saw the llama,
it spit on her sweatshirt hood
and that was funny.*

*I loved to go to Florida to visit her,
and whenever we went
Nanny always made me laugh.
Whenever Nanny came to Youngstown
she always stayed at the Holiday Inn at night,
but in the day she came to my house.
I had very much fun with Nanny
and I wish we could have
spent more time together.*

With Gerald Ford (above left).

Surprise 40th Wedding Anniversary celebration with Corky and Gene Ribakoff (above right).

Our family (right).

Our yacht trip with the Ribakoffs, Nessels, and Greenbergs. (below left).

Bud and Barbara Levinson (below right).

Part Four
Conclusion

Conclusion

Chapter Sixteen
Continuing my Education

A few months after Bernita died, I couldn't face spending my summer alone and I wanted a brief respite from my Palm Beach life. I thought that spending the summer at a university would help me focus on something other than my memories so I went to see my friend and mentor, Tana Ebbole.

Tana and I have worked together for a long time and she allows me to be a part of her planning and incorporates my interests. When I went to see her, she was involved in planning a new independent agency that

Chapter Sixteen
Continuing my Education

would oversee the proper administration of non-profit social service agencies, especially those receiving community funds. Too many agencies had either poor administrative policies or were experiencing severe financial problems due to improper management. She asked me to participate in the planning process and suggested that we seek out a college program that offered the type of training that would enable me to better assist her.

We settled on Brandeis University which is located outside of Boston, Massachusetts. I have a special warmth for Brandeis because it is an unusual place in this cockeyed world. It welcomes people from all over the world who wish to acquire skills that will help them improve their communities. It is a nonsectarian university founded in 1948 under Jewish sponsorship.

I enrolled in a seven-week MBA course in non-profit management and it was not a walk in the park. I was competing with students from around the world. In fact, I got a "C" on my first paper. It was distressing, but I rallied when I finally understood the objectives of my professor. Her approach to solving problems differed from my business approach and the use of financial resources to solve problems.

My class had people from India, Russia, Africa, and all over Europe. We exchanged ideas and I gained a new awareness of how social service is practiced in the rest of the world. I loved that experience.

I also took a course that focused on ways to evaluate the efficiency of social programs. What I learned in that course changed the way I practice my social advocacy. I realized that too many programs sound good, look good and satisfy people temporarily, but in too many cases, they provide no long-lasting effective outcomes. Today, I expect to see long-term positive outcomes for the programs we are funding. The days of "feel-good" programs are gone.

After completing my course at Brandeis, I returned to Palm Beach County and began working with Tana, Suzette Wexner, executive director of the Palm HealthCare Foundation, and Scott Badesch and Alexandria Douglas-Bartolone from the United Way, in developing the new agency. It was successfully established and I am very pleased to have been a part of the effort.

Chapter Seventeen
My Eightieth Birthday

Happy 80th Birthday! (left to right: Randy Palo, Jeanette Hartzell, Tracey Lamport, Bud, Pat McNamara, Jacqui Nicholson, Cindy Bartosek, Terry Jurewicz, and Bob Palin (in back).

I have a habit of counting the days before important things are about to happen in my life. It could be a vacation, a party I am hosting, or a birthday I am celebrating. Reaching a milestone, such as one's eightieth birthday, is an even bigger reason to count the days. Yet it somehow worried me that I was now reaching my eightieth year and no one in my immediate family had ever lived that long.

Although I realize that lifespans in the United States have increased in the past thirty years, it was no comfort looking at my family's history. I really didn't think I would die before I reached this milestone, but I am superstitious. On August 6, 2006, it came to pass and I celebrated my eightieth birthday.

Prior to my birthday, I had a feeling that my buddies at work would plan something to honor that date. I have been close to them, particularly Jeanette Hartzell, who has never let a five-year birthday pass without some type of acknowledgement. She never said a word to me, but I became suspicious when a few months prior to my birthday, my good friends, Seth Bernstein and Nate Nichols set up a dinner date. I often had lunch with them, but dinner was another issue. I thought something was fishy, but decided not to question anyone about it. Discretion was called for.

As my birthday approached, no one was making plans to celebrate with me. I realized something had been planned when Jeanette asked me when I was returning from my weekend trip to Santa Fe, New Mexico. When I told her that I was coming in at midnight on July 17th, she said she hoped I wouldn't be too tired on July 18th. That was my defining clue. I didn't know what was happening, where it was happening, or who was involved, but I was pretty sure that I was going to be entertained.

Seth Bernstein, Nate Nicols, and Debi Stewart.

I left the office early on July 18th and asked Jeanette what I should wear for that evening. She asked me why I was questioning her and I told her I knew something was happening. I really knew nothing more about the evening, but I wanted to be prepared. Well, I was scheduled to meet Seth and Nate at the Children's Services Council and then go to dinner. When I met Seth, he told me that we were going to dinner in Lake Worth at a new restaurant they thought I would like called the Jetsetter Lounge.

My friends and co-workers.

On the way, Seth received a phone call, and I knew he was faking his responses, but I feigned ignorance. When I realized that we were passing the address of the restaurant, I said, "Wait a minute, you are passing it by." He said, "Really, how could I miss it," and turned the car around a few blocks later. He needed to stall our arrival because one of our guests was going to be a little late.

Being roasted by Delorisa Brown with Jean Malecki.

149

Chapter Seventeen

Note the vest on the cake.

Cornesha Dukes Chisholm.

Honestly, that is all I knew. When we entered the restaurant, I naturally expressed surprise, but the real shock was that seventy friends and co-workers, all from my past endeavors in the community, were there to greet me. I cannot tell you how thrilled and pleased I was to be so embraced and honored by so many of the people I had worked with over the years. I was truly taken aback. Having so many friends present was the real surprise.

People from all over the county attended. It was wonderful to be recognized and roasted by all of these good people, too many to mention here. The warmth and feelings expressed by the people who spoke made that evening an event I will remember for the rest of my life.

I was "roasted" by many of the guests, including representatives from some of the agencies that I worked with. One agency from Pahokee, Florida, represented by my friend, Cornesha Dukes Chisholm, gave me a plaque with a key to the city and an "Honorary Pahokee Blue Devil" t-shirt. I was also honored with a presentation by Delorisa Brown, the principal of Barton Elementary, with whom I had worked to create educational programs. She presented me with a punch bowl, paid for by one of the students I had taught in our English class. So many friends and colleagues talked about the work we had done together, that my tears were flowing like wine.

Scott Badesch reminded me that I was always difficult, but always seemed to be the "conscience of the community." I truly value that description of my work. In fact, I strive for that goal every day. If I could have that sentiment written on my tombstone, I would be honored.

I am unable to mention all of the people who spoke that night, and most of them were very funny discussing me and my impulsiveness, but I was deeply touched by the entire evening. I really appreciated everyone's efforts, especially Jacqui Nicholson, Tracey Lamport, Michael Lascasas, and my close friend, Jeanette Hartzell. The celebration made me feel that my work and my efforts are worthwhile and appreciated. It was a truly wonderful evening.

Enjoying a roast from Debbie Labella.

The culmination of my eightieth birthday was a trip to Alaska with my entire family and my son Jon's friend, Bob Oppenheimer. We all met in Vancouver, British Columbia, the day before my birthday, to prepare for a seven-day cruise aboard the Celebrity Cruise ship, the *Infinity*. I had never been on such a large vessel.

Alaska Cruise.

Chapter Seventeen

My son Jon and I ready to board the ship.

There were over two thousand passengers on board and the ship's crew handled all of the people amazingly well. The first night we sailed was my actual birthday, August 6th. My children arranged a special champagne birthday celebration. It was wonderful. I was thrilled at what they had done and the toasts that each one of them made to me.

The natural beauty of Alaska is something I will always remember. We visited nature sites, viewed the glaciers, and saw many of the wonderful animals that you see only in pictures. The ship offered many opportunities for adventure and we did everything, including taking a helicopter ride that landed on a glacier. Our guide explained how the glaciers formed and how they are affected by global warming. Although it was the beginning of August, it was so cold. We were thrilled when the helicopter picked us up forty minutes later.

On one day of the cruise, most of us took a seaplane to view Alaska's fjords, while Jeffrey and Joe spent the entire afternoon fishing with a guide. They had a great time catching the fish, cooking them, and then eating them. They returned to the ship exhausted. We also watched the salmon, which was a real experience in itself. All in all, it was a wonderful trip that none of us will ever forget. It was such a privilege to be with my family celebrating my eightieth birthday and spending that valuable time with them.

On the glacier with Jeff, Nick, and Joe (above, center).

Helicopter ride back to the ship (above).

Birthday Toasts, clockwise from left: Nick, Jeff, Joe, Jenny, and family toast.

What a wonderful way to celebrate my 80th birthday. From left: Bob, Jeff, Cathy, Bud, Nick, and Jon.

Chapter Eighteen
This is what it's all about, Buddy!

It has been over two years since Bernita passed away and I am now getting reconciled to the fact that she is no longer with me physically. My friends tell me I should get on with my life. They tell me it isn't normal to live the way I am living, without a mate, not being part of the crowd. While I understand what they are saying, I am not willing to change my current lifestyle.

My life as an eighty-year-old codger is actually pretty cool. My health is fine; I exercise daily and racewalk about four miles, three times a week. I have a physical fitness trainer, Molly Ragsdale, who supervises my work in the gym and in the pool. When I'm home in Palm Beach, I work as a volunteer every day, and love what I do. I play golf every Saturday and Sunday, mostly with my friend Irwin Levy and our regular foursome. Yes, I would love to have a female companion, but she would need to be a special kind of woman; one who is independent, clever, and not in need of a daily companion because my work and the schedule I keep is not that of the average retired man.

I was married to a fantastic woman with a tremendous sense of humor. Bernita was the one person who knew that my true talents were never utilized as a businessman. Her encouragement helped me become the person I am today. If there is a woman who could improve the life I am leading, I would be very interested, but I intend to maintain my current pace as long as I am able. After living alone for a while, with my own thoughts, I have reached a different plateau in my thinking; and I am somehow convinced that I was put on earth to live the life I am leading today.

Since Bernita's death, my world has changed. I am a single parent and it is a tremendous responsibility. Bernita was a phenomenal mother, a good listener, and not at all an interfering kind of parent. It was not an easy role for me to assume.

Bernita always told me that I lectured everyone too much, but I guess that's the way it is. I am trying to follow her pattern. I work hard to honor her wishes that her sons remain friendly with one another and maintain close contact although they have busy lives. We have been blessed with a fantastic daughter-in-law, Cathy, who continues to insure that Bernita's wishes are fulfilled; and we have our friend Bob, who cares deeply about our son Jon and really became part of our family during our summer trip to Alaska.

My grandkids are absolutely great. My granddaughter, Jenny, who is now sixteen, is working and driving her own car. She's not only pretty, she is a knockout, and a very nice gal. She is a very good student and is currently thinking about college choices and a career. Jenny is a wonderful girl and was a great help to her mother, Cathy, when she went back to school to pursue her nursing degree.

My grandsons, Joe and Nick, are equally wonderful. They are good students and I have great hopes for their futures. The boys are very involved with sports, especially baseball. I hope I have created memories for them that they will always treasure, especially after our special family trip to Alaska. I know I will never forget it. I hope to share many more things with them.

My hope for each of you, my sons and my grandchildren, is that you follow your own dreams and don't settle for less than what you are capable of doing. My wish is that you find work that you're passionate about because passion creates satisfaction and self-fulfillment. If you have no passion for what you are doing, then it's time to change your direction.

It is not easy. There are many roadblocks along the way and you must learn to be resilient. Don't remain stuck on old ideas when new opportunities appear. Don't get hung up on who you are and what you know. Always be ready to learn new things and assume new challenges. I am eighty years old and I am so pleased that I continue to study and to learn every day.

Never, and I mean never, take yourself too seriously. Always strive to learn and be better. Make up your own mind. Build a better mousetrap. Learn to be conservative with your thoughts and actions. Don't blow all your money or your intellectual reserves. Keep something for a rainy day. As Grandpa Joe Ungar used to say, "Money flows away from you as easily as it flows towards you." Bernita and I watched ourselves, we were conservative, and it made for a good life. We always knew who we were, where we were going, and in our own little way, we always arrived there. Learn to take special advice from responsible and honorable mentors and use it carefully. While I wish you financial success, remember that true success comes when you are happy doing something worthwhile and meaningful.

Chapter Eighteen

Above all, you must learn to be charitable with both your thoughts and your finances. Give of your time and money to things you believe in. It is very important that in your efforts you teach others how to help themselves. I hope that each of you develops a charitable personality; it is part of the legacy Bernita and I leave to you. Remember that the rewarding thing about charity is that it is the giver who receives the larger gift.

My dear family, I want you to know that you are my life. It is hard for me to finish this review of my eighty years because I am a cockeyed optimist, and I know that I have many more things to accomplish, many more people to meet, and many more happy times to spend with you. My hope is that all of you search for good things and enjoy a happy, peaceful and fruitful life. That is my prayer and my wish for you.

Shalom,

BT

Jenny, Poppy, and Baby Joe.

Nicky and Cathy.

Jenny, Joe, and Baby Nicky.

Nicky and Jeff.

Two young brothers, Joe and Nicky.

Growing up, Nick and Joe on our Alaska cruise.

UW Volunteer of the Year Award.

Jeff, Jenny, Cathy, Nick, & Joe.

My beautiful girls, Cathy and Jenny.

Jenny and Joe.

I love our grandchildren: Jenny, Nick, and Joe.

Our handsome son, Jon.

Jenny

Joe

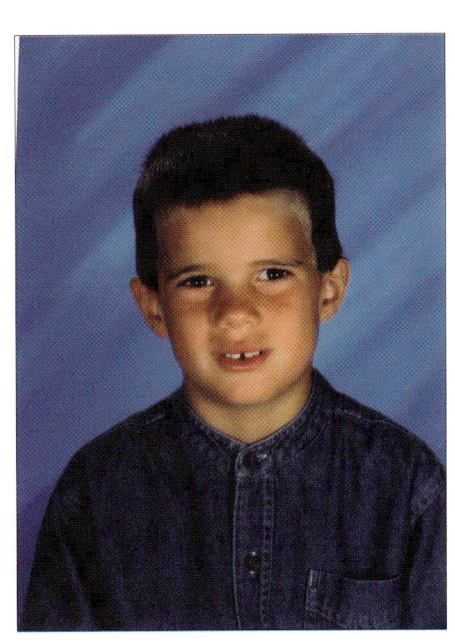

Nick

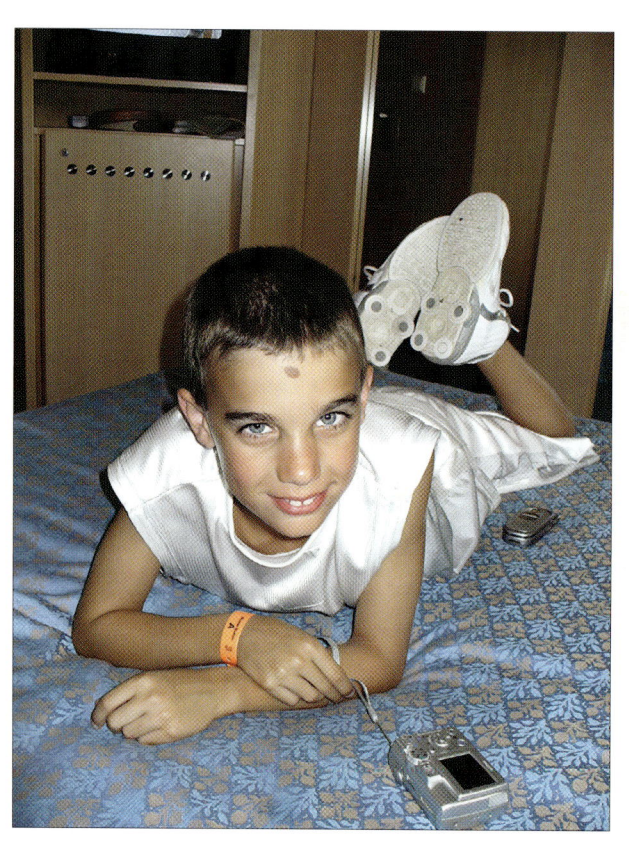

Check out the mustache; with Bernita and Fran.

Enjoying life with Bernita.

Beginning of my fine golf career.

Still "dressed in white."

My cousin, Bert Pincus.

Bert Lockshin and Bernita.

Bernita and her two favorite things, smoking and Las Vegas.

Aboard the "Chunnel," the Channel Tunnel Train that connects England and France.

Bernita at the All-Star game with Lita Fromstein (center) and Sue Seling.

Painting the mural at our Leverett House oceanview apartment.

Yachting on the Mediterranean with Burt and Barbara Stern.

A very special gift from my friend, Dale Anderson, a handmade belt representing children and a kiss on the cheek.

Race-walking keeps a busy guy like me in shape.

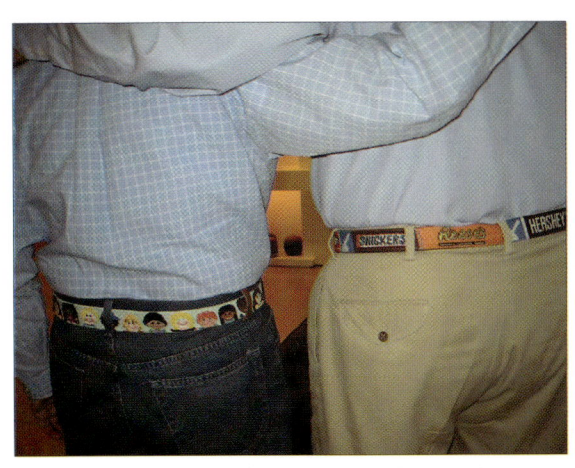
Doug Anderson and I show off our belts.

Being interviewed with Dan Shorter about our work on hunger.

My buddy and lunch companion, Steve Levin.

Jeanette Freeman Hartzell and I "step-up" to physical fitness.

Dr. Jean Malecki and Dr. Alina Alonso.

The talented Michael Lascasas created the cover artwork for my book.

Two fake photos displayed at my 80th birthday party: Conversing with Steve Jobs and Bill Gates; and Golda Meir.